Jean Martin

T0344215

Core
Biology

CAMBRIDGE
UNIVERSITY PRESS

Series editors	Bryan Milner
	Jean Martin
	John Mills
Biology editor	Jean Martin
Core Science authors	Jenifer Burden
	Paul Butler
	Zoë Crompton
	Sam Ellis
	Peter Evans
	Jean Martin
	John Mills
	Bryan Milner
Consultants	Kate Chaytor
	Nigel Heslop
	Martyn Keeley

CAMBRIDGE
UNIVERSITY PRESS

University Printing House, Cambridge CB2 8BS, United Kingdom

One Liberty Plaza, 20th Floor, New York, NY 10006, USA

477 Williamstown Road, Port Melbourne, VIC 3207, Australia

314–321, 3rd Floor, Plot 3, Splendor Forum, Jasola District Centre, New Delhi – 110025, India

103 Penang Road, #05-06/07, Visioncrest Commercial, Singapore 238467

Cambridge University Press is part of the University of Cambridge.

It furthers the University's mission by disseminating knowledge in the pursuit of education, learning and research at the highest international levels of excellence.

www.cambridge.org
Information on this title: www.cambridge.org/9780521666398

© Cambridge University Press 1999

First published 1999

20 19

Printed in Great Britain by CPI Group (UK) Ltd, Croydon CR0 4YY

A catalogue record for this publication is available from the British Library

ISBN 978-0-521-66639-8 Paperback

Cambridge University Press has no responsibility for the persistence or accuracy of URLs for external or third-party internet websites referred to in this publication, and does not guarantee that any content on such websites is, or will remain, accurate or appropriate. Information regarding prices, travel timetables, and other factual information given in this work is correct at the time of first printing but Cambridge University Press does not guarantee the accuracy of such information thereafter.

Cover photo: Ragweed pollen © Carolina Biological Supp/Phototake NYC, Robert Harding Picture Library

Contents

How this book is organised

Core Biology is designed to cover the biology (AT2) component of the National Curriculum for Science at Key Stage 3. It also covers the biology requirement of the Common Entrance Examination at 13+.

For most pupils, Key Stage 3 comprises the first three years (Years 7, 8 and 9) of their secondary education, culminating in the Key Stage 3 SATs towards the end of Year 9.

If these pupils are to do themselves justice in the SATs tests, they really need to have made significant, recent use of all the scientific ideas that they might encounter in the SATs.

To ensure that this happens, the content of *Core Biology* is organised as follows.

BASIC CONCEPTS [for all pupils, normally in Years 7 and 8]	CONSOLIDATION [for all pupils, normally in Year 9]	+	DEVELOPMENT [for some pupils, normally in Year 9]
This section of the book:	This section of the book:		These additional (Core+) pages, at the end of each topic in the Consolidation section:
■ covers the great majority of concepts needed for KS3 SATs up to Level 6;	■ revisits all the Basic Concepts, in different contexts and at a quicker pace;		■ extend basic concepts further and/or apply them to more difficult contexts;
■ introduces new ideas gently, one at a time, with ample opportunity for pupils to confirm their mastery of each new idea immediately after it is introduced.	■ extends them, where necessary, so that pupils are fully prepared for KS3 SATs up to Level 6.		■ prepare pupils for KS3 SATs up to Level 7.

Pages 8 and 9 are set out so that they show where each concept area in the Basic Concepts section is Consolidated and further Developed.

They show, for example, that:

Basic concepts about plant nutrition are covered in:	The basic concepts are consolidated and extended a little in:	The ideas are further developed and applied to other contexts in:
3.8 How do plants grow? 3.9 Minerals for plant growth 3.10 How do plants take in what they need?	C3.2 Photosynthesis: a detective story C3.3 Growing tomato plants without soil	C3.9 More discoveries about photosynthesis C3.10 Growing enough food

The links between the different sections are shown at the top of the relevant pages of the book.

It should be noted that *Core Biology* does <u>not</u> attempt to cover the additional content that may be required for the SATs Extension papers. The additional material needed to answer some of these questions in these papers derives from part of the Programme of Study specified by the National Curriculum for Key Stage 4. Teachers who feel that their pupils are ready for this material in Year 9 are advised to use the relevant parts of textbooks written to support Key Stage 4.

Pupils' notes

The text is liberally sprinkled with questions designed to provide pupil interaction and allow them to confirm their mastery of ideas as they are presented. The outcomes of these questions are <u>not</u> intended to result in a coherent set of notes for revision – this is the purpose of the summary sections (see below).

Some of these questions have a magnifier symbol printed alongside. This indicates that the answer to the question <u>cannot</u> be found in the text. Pupils are expected to find out the answer from elsewhere.

A 'working notebook' for answering these text questions is recommended. This notebook might also be used for any other written work which is not intended to form a permanent record for revision purposes, such as some aspects of practical work, answers to questions from Question banks in the *Supplementary Materials*, etc.

The **key** words in each spread are highlighted in **bold**. Pupils use these words to complete the summary sections headed *What you need to remember* (WYNTR). The accumulated set of WYNTR passages comprises a record of the knowledge and understanding that pupils will need for SATs.

A separate notebook for WYNTR summaries is recommended. This will make a useful reference for revision.

Since they are to be used for revision, it is, of course, essential that pupils' completed summaries are correct. These are supplied at the back of *Core Biology* and can be used for checking.

Practical work

The content and presentation of any particular piece of practical work will depend on what the teacher considers are the main aims of that practical assignment, e.g. to make otherwise abstract ideas more concrete and meaningful or to develop and assess Sc1 skills and abilities. Consequently, practical work on a particular topic may vary considerably. So, though *Core Biology* helps to develop Sc1 skills and abilities by presenting information about investigations for pupils to interpret and evaluate, detailed instructions for pupils' practical work are <u>not</u> provided. It is assumed that the teacher will provide the practical work to support topics that best suits the needs of their pupils.

The text of *Core Biology* has also been presented in a way that does not depend on practical work; it is completely stand-alone.

Supplementary materials

Core Biology Supplementary Materials are available to support the pupils' text. This fully photocopiable resource assists teaching and lesson-planning by providing practical suggestions, tests, worksheets (for homework or class use) and answers to all the questions in the pupils' text. There is also a matching grid to show how *Core Biology* covers the Key Stage 3 Science National Curriculum.

These materials comprise:

- a *Commentary* for each double-page spread of the pupils' text which includes:
  - full details of the expected *Outcomes to questions* in the text, written in language that pupils themselves are expected to use;
  - *Suggestions for practical activities*;
- *Worksheets* wherever these are particularly useful;
- *Topic tests* and *Question banks*.

The Common Entrance Examination at 13+

Pupils preparing for the Common Entrance Examination at 13+ will need to have covered the material in *Core Biology* a year earlier than pupils preparing for SATs.

This can be achieved via several different approaches:

- embarking on *Core Biology* a year earlier (e.g. in the preparatory school sector);
- covering the Basic Concepts section in a single year and proceeding to the Consolidation and Development section the following year;
- visiting each topic area <u>once only</u> in a two-year programme, i.e. covering the Basic Concepts section and then the Consolidation and Development section end on to each other. When using this strategy, only selected aspects of the Consolidation material may be needed and the remainder omitted.

Ways through this book

The word 'CORE+' appears at the top of the Development pages as a reminder that they are needed only for the higher-tier Key Stage 3 SATs.

1.1 What can living things do?

Suzy and her dog do not look the same. But they do have a lot in common. This is because they are both <u>living things</u>.

1 Look at the pictures. Then write down <u>three</u> things that are the same about Suzy and her dog.

*Suzy and her dog both **move** about.*

*Suzy and her dog can see, hear, feel and smell. We say that they can **sense** things.*

*Suzy and her dog were once much smaller. They both **grow**.*

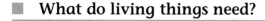
What do living things need?

Suzy's brother David has a cat. To stay alive David and his cat need to feed and to breathe.

2 Write down <u>two</u> reasons why David and his cat need food.

3 Copy and complete the sentence:

To get energy from food, David and his cat also need _____.

*David and his cat both eat **food**. They need this to grow and to move.*

oxygen

*To get energy from food, David and his cat both need **oxygen** from the air.*

■ Getting rid of waste

The children and their pets need to get rid of **waste** from their bodies. If they don't get rid of this waste, it will poison them.

4 Write down <u>two</u> kinds of waste they must get rid of.

Air gets extra carbon dioxide.

The children and their pets get rid of carbon dioxide. They also get rid of waste in their urine.

■ What else must living things do?

David's cat has had kittens. These will still be alive when his cat gets old and dies.

David may become a father when he grows up, and Suzy might have children too.

5 Copy and complete the sentences.

All living things eventually _____.
So some of each kind have to produce young.
We say that they _____.

All animals are alive. They all do the same things as the children and their pets.

We call these things **life processes**.

Plants are alive too. You can read about their life processes on pages 14–15.

*Living things produce young like themselves. We say that they **reproduce**.*

WHAT YOU NEED TO REMEMBER (Copy and complete using the **key words**)

What can living things do?

All animals:
- ■ _____, _____ and _____;
- ■ take in _____ and _____;
- ■ get rid of _____;
- ■ and _____.

We call these things _____ _____.

More about life processes: C1.3

1.2 Is it alive?

To see if something is **alive**, we look at what it does.

- If we can find **all** of the life processes, then it's alive.

- If we can't find all the life processes, then it's not alive. We say that it is **non-living**.

1 Copy and complete the sentence.

Things that are alive show _____ of the life processes.

Stones and stonechats

Stonechats are small birds. They perch on stone walls, bushes and telephone wires in the countryside.

2 **(a)** Copy and complete the table.

Does it ... ?	Stonechat	Stone
sense	yes	no
move		
grow		
take in food		
take in oxygen		
get rid of waste		
reproduce		

(b) Is the stone alive? Give reasons for your answer.

3 **(a)** Make a similar table for a horse and a rocking horse.

(b) Is the rocking horse alive? Give reasons for your answer.

> **REMEMBER** from page 11
>
> All animals
> - sense, move and grow;
> - take in food and oxygen;
> - get rid of waste;
> - reproduce.
>
> These things are called <u>life processes</u>.

male stonechat

female stonechat

Aeroplanes and birds

Aeroplanes look much more alive than stones or rocking horses, and pilots often talk to them as if they were alive.

The plane gives out waste gases.

The plane needs fuel and oxygen to provide energy.

Lights go on automatically when its dark.

The plane moves through the air.

4 (a) Look at the diagram. Then copy and complete the table.

Does it ... ?	Bird	Aeroplane
sense	yes	
move	yes	
grow	yes	no, they are full size when we first make them
take in food	yes	in a way; fuel is like food, but we have to put the fuel in
take in oxygen	yes	
get rid of waste	yes	
reproduce	yes	

(b) Is the plane alive? Give reasons for your answers.

Robots

This robot can find items in the warehouse that people need. So can the warehouse person.

The robot uses sensors to find its way around and to find what it has been sent to get.

When you watch the robot, you'd think it was alive.

5 (a) What <u>two</u> life processes does the robot show?

(b) What life processes are <u>not</u> shown by the robot?

WHAT YOU NEED TO REMEMBER (Copy and complete using the **key words**)

Is it alive?

Some things have never been _____ . We say they are _____ .

They sometimes show some of the life processes, but they don't show _____ of them.

More about life processes: C1.3

1.3 Plants are alive

It isn't just animals that are alive.

Plants are alive too. We can tell this by looking at what plants do.

1 Look at the pictures. Then write down <u>five</u> things that plants can do which animals do too.

REMEMBER from page 11

Animals:

- sense, move and grow;
- take in food and oxygen;
- get rid of waste;
- reproduce.

These things are called life processes.

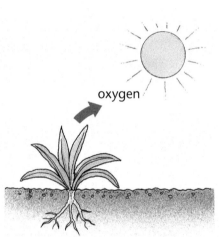

*Plants **reproduce**. Seeds **grow** into new plants.*

*Plants can **sense** where the light is. They can grow or **move** to face the light.*

*Plants get rid of **waste**.*

Plants can move

Plants can't move about like animals can.

But parts of plants can move, for example to face the Sun. Other parts of some plants can also move.

Venus fly trap.

2 Look at the photos of the Venus fly trap.

   (a) Which part of the plant moves?

   (b) When does this happen?

   (c) The Venus fly trap, like other plants, can't move about. Why not?

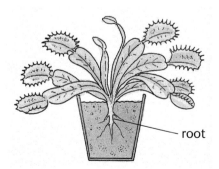

root

Plants can make food

Plants are different from animals because they can make their own food.

The diagrams show what they need to do this.

3 Copy and complete the table.

What the plant needs to make food	Where the plant gets it from

The substances a plant needs to make food are called **nutrients**.

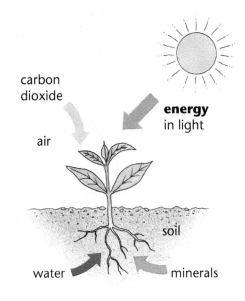

carbon dioxide

energy in light

air

water   minerals

soil

What a plant needs to make food.

Important parts of plants

The different parts of plants do different **jobs**.

4 Look at the diagram. Then copy and complete the table.

Part of plant	What is its job?
flower	
stem	
leaf	
root	
bud	

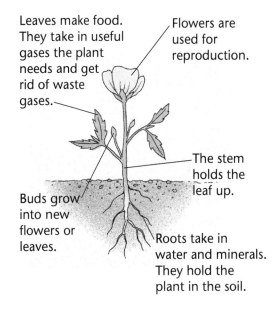

Leaves make food. They take in useful gases the plant needs and get rid of waste gases.

Flowers are used for reproduction.

The stem holds the leaf up.

Buds grow into new flowers or leaves.

Roots take in water and minerals. They hold the plant in the soil.

The different parts of a plant are called **organs**.

WHAT YOU NEED TO REMEMBER (Copy and complete using the **key words**)

Plants are alive

Plants, like animals, are living things.
They _____, _____, _____, _____ and get rid of _____.

Plants make their own food using _____ from sunlight and _____ from the soil and air.

Different parts of a plant do different _____.
The different parts of a plant are called _____.

More about life processes: C1.3

1.4 Important parts of your body

REMEMBER from page 15

Different parts of plants are called organs. Each organ does a different job.

Like plants, your body has many different parts called **organs**. Different organs of your body do different jobs.

For example, your stomach helps your body break down your food. But your stomach does not do this on its own!

Several organs work together to break down your food. Because they digest your food, we call them your **digestive** system.

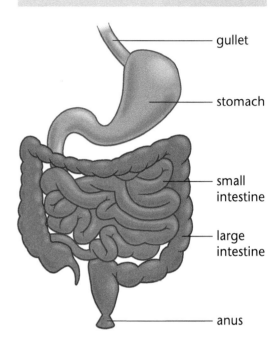

The digestive system.

■ Your digestive system

The diagram shows some of the organs in your digestive system.

1 Copy and complete the sentence.

Organs in the digestive system include the _____, stomach, small _____, _____ intestine and anus.

■ Your nervous system

There are other groups of organs in your body. We call one group the **nervous** system.

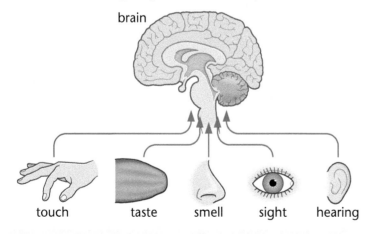

2 List <u>three</u> organs in the nervous system.

3 What life process does the nervous system carry out?

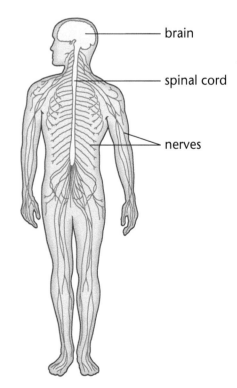

The nervous system.

Your circulatory system

All the organs in your body need food and oxygen.

They all produce waste which needs to be taken away.

Your **circulatory** system carries food, oxygen and wastes around your body.

4 Write down the names of <u>three</u> parts of the circulatory system.

5 Copy and complete the sentences.

The circulatory system carries _____ and _____ to all parts of the body.

It also carries _____ from all parts of the body.

Your body has many other organs. These organs work together in what we call organ **systems**.

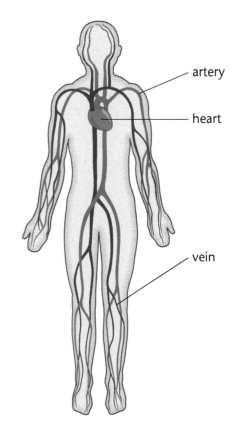

The circulatory system.

WHAT YOU NEED TO REMEMBER (Copy and complete using the **key words**)

Important parts of your body

The different parts of your body are called _____. These work together in groups called organ _____.

Some organ systems in your body

Organ system	What it does
_____ system	carries food, oxygen and wastes around your body
_____ system	tells you what's happening around you
_____ system	breaks down food so your body can use it

You should also be able to name the organs belonging to each organ system in the table.
Your body has other organ systems too.
You will learn about some of these later.

More about organs: C1.2

1.5 The smallest parts of animals and plants

Animals and plants are made up of parts called organs. These organs are made up of lots of even smaller bits called **cells**.

Cells from your cheek

Emma has scraped off a tiny piece from the inside of her cheek. You can see what her cheek lining looks like using a <u>microscope</u>.

Microscopes make small things look a lot bigger. We say that they <u>magnify</u> them.

1 Look at the photograph of the magnified cheek lining. Describe what it looks like.

2 What do we call each small bit of the cheek lining?

How big are cells?

Cells are very small.

Big animals and plants are made up of millions and millions of cells. The bigger an animal or plant is, the more cells it has.

3 Look at the diagram of a cheek cell. How many cheek cells would fit end to end in a space of 1 millimetre?

4 Look at the animals in the pictures. Write down their names in order of how many cells they have. Start with the animal that has the <u>most</u> cells.

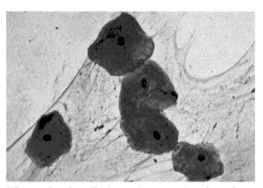

These cheek cells have been stained so they show up easily.

$\frac{1}{100}$ of a millimetre

The space between these lines is 1 millimetre.

Cheek cell.

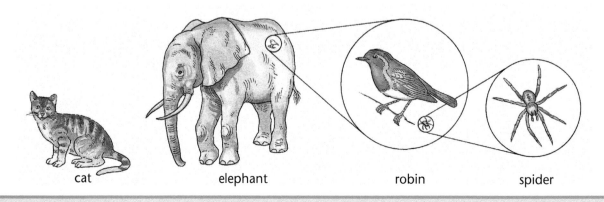

cat   elephant   robin   spider

Each part of a cell has a different job

Most animal cells have the same basic parts. The diagram shows what these parts are.

5 Copy and complete the table to show what different parts of a cell do.

Cell part	What it does
nucleus	
cell membrane	
cytoplasm	

The **nucleus** controls what happens in the cell.

The **cell membrane** controls what passes in and out of the cell.

Most of the cell's reactions happen in the **cytoplasm**.

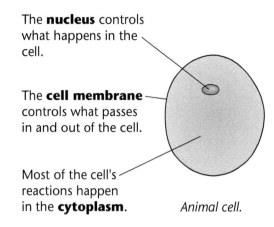

Animal cell.

Plant cells

Plant cells have the same parts as animal cells. They also have some parts that animal cells do not have.

cell **wall** (strong and rigid to support the cell)

cell membrane

vacuole filled with cell sap (water, salts and sugars)

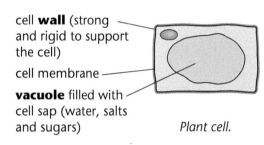

Plant cell.

6 Copy the diagram of a plant cell. Label the nucleus, cytoplasm and cell membrane.

7 What parts does a plant cell have that an animal cell doesn't?

8 Look at the four different kinds of cells, A, B, C and D. For each one, say whether it is an animal cell or a plant cell.

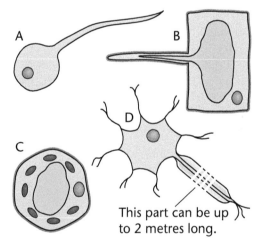

A

B

C

D

This part can be up to 2 metres long.

WHAT YOU NEED TO REMEMBER (Copy and complete using the **key words**)

The smallest parts of animals and plants

All plants and animals are made up of tiny bits called _____.

All cells have:
- a _____ which controls what happens in a cell;
- _____ where most chemical reactions take place;
- a _____ _____ which controls what goes in and out of a cell.

Plant cells also have a cell _____ and a _____.

More about cells: C1.1

1.6 Microbes

REMEMBER from page 18

Microscopes magnify what you are looking at. They make things look a lot bigger than they really are.

All living things are made from very tiny cells. Large animals and plants are made from lots and lots of cells. The smallest living things are made from just one cell.

The photo shows a living thing which has only one cell. It is very **small**.

You can only see it using a **microscope**, so we call it a microbe or micro-organism.

1 Why can a microscope help us to see this microbe?

2 Copy and complete the table.

Word	What does it mean?
micro_____	This magnifies what you are looking at.
micro-_____ or microbe	You cannot see these organisms with your eyes alone.

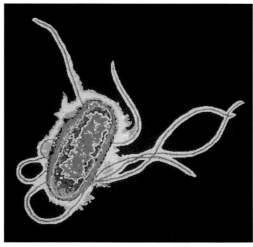

This is an E. coli bacterium. It is magnified 4000 times.

▇ Where are microbes?

Microbes are all around us. They are in our air, food, water and our bodies!

Bacteria are one kind of microbe. This student is trying to find out if there are any bacteria in river water.

3 Why can't we see the bacteria in water?

4 Why can we see the bacteria from the water sample after two days?

Notice that we say:

■ bacterium when there is one.
■ bacteria when there are more than one.

This colony has millions of bacteria in it.

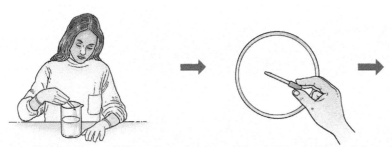

This water is from a river.

The jelly in this dish is food for microbes.

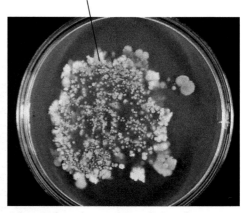

After 2 days in a warm place, the microbes have reproduced lots of times.

Some microbes are harmful

Gary is not feeling very well. He has a bad cold.

Colds are caused by microbes even smaller than bacteria. These microbes are called <u>viruses</u>.

Different viruses and some bacteria can cause other **diseases**.

The diagram shows what happens when Gary catches the cold then gets better again.

5 Write down the following sentences in order to tell the story of Gary's cold.

- He gets better.

- He feels ill.

- A few cold viruses get into his body.

- His body destroys the viruses.

- The viruses reproduce very fast inside his cells.

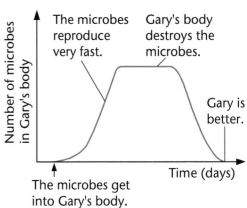

The microbes reproduce very fast.

Gary's body destroys the microbes.

Gary is better.

Number of microbes in Gary's body

Time (days)

The microbes get into Gary's body.

Some microbes are useful

Some microbes are very useful. The pictures show some places where microbes are needed.

6 Copy and complete the table.

Where microbes are needed	What the microbes do
in a bakery	
in a sewage treatment plant	
in a dairy	
in a cow's stomach	

Yeast is a microbe that makes bread rise.

Microbes in the cow's stomach help it to digest grass.

Microbes feed on **sewage**. *They break it down into harmless substances.*

Microbes turn milk into yogurt and cheese

WHAT YOU NEED TO REMEMBER (Copy and complete using the **key words**)

Microbes

Microbes are everywhere. They are so _____ we need a_____ to see them.

Some microbes are useful. For example, they can break down _____.

Other microbes are harmful. They can cause _____ in animals and plants.

1.7 Sorting out living things

REMEMBER from page 11

All living things
- grow;
- sense;
- move;
- get rid of waste;
- reproduce.

All living things are alike in many ways. But some living things are more alike than others.

1 Write down <u>five</u> ways in which all living things are alike.

2 Look at the pictures. Then write down <u>three</u> ways that a dog, a cat and a mouse are like each other but different from a snail.

There are millions of different kinds of living things.

It is easier for us to study living things if we sort them into **groups** which have lots of things in common.

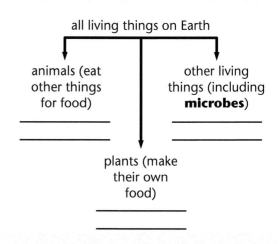

■ Three very big groups

You have already been sorting living things into groups, in pages 10–21.

The diagram shows you what these main groups are.

3 Copy the diagram on the right.

Look at the following pictures of <u>six</u> living things. Then write their names under the correct headings on your diagram.

all living things on Earth

animals (eat other things for food)
_____
_____

other living things (including **microbes**)
_____
_____

plants (make their own food)
_____
_____

lion

dandelion

oak tree

bacterial cell

killer whale

yeast cell

Different ways of sorting animals

The three main groups can be sorted into smaller groups. For example, there are many different ways of sorting out animals into smaller groups.

4 Sort the animals on this page into three groups depending on where they live. Give each group a heading:

Live in water	Live on land	Can fly

5 Now use a different way to sort out the animals into groups. (Hint: You might like to try using the number of legs.)

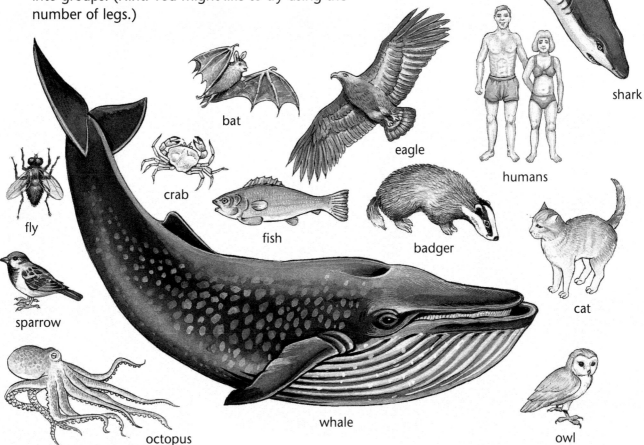

horse

spider

hamster

shark

bat

eagle

humans

crab

fish

badger

fly

cat

sparrow

octopus

whale

owl

WHAT YOU NEED TO REMEMBER (Copy and complete using the **key words**)

Sorting out living things

We sort out all living things into _____. Plants and animals are two main groups.

Some living things, including _____, do not fit into these two groups.

More about classification: C1.7

1.8 What is it?

On pages 22–23, you found out that you can sort living things into groups.

One way of doing this is to use a <u>key</u>.

Cat.

Pine tree.

A simple key

This is how to use a key to find which group the living things in the pictures belong to.

- Go to the start of the key.

- When you come to a branch, choose which way to go.

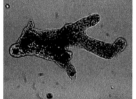
Amoeba. x100

Ant.

For example, for the cat you choose these branches:

- made of many cells;

- has no green parts;

- has four legs.

1 Make a copy of the key.

Use the key to find out which group the tree, the ant and the amoeba belong to. Then write their names in the boxes.

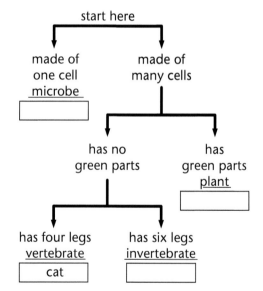

start here

made of one cell
<u>microbe</u>
[ ]

made of many cells

has no green parts

has green parts
<u>plant</u>
[ ]

has four legs
<u>vertebrate</u>
[cat]

has six legs
<u>invertebrate</u>
[ ]

Another way of writing this key

A key can also be written as a list of questions.

2 Copy the key below. Then complete the missing parts.

1 { made of one cell   _____
   { made of many cells   go to 2

2 { has green parts   *plant*
   { has no green parts   go to 3

3 { has four legs   _____
   { ___ ___ ___   *invertebrate*

DID YOU KNOW?

Animals can be split into two smaller groups:
- vertebrates (with bones);
- invertebrates (without bones).

You will learn more about these groups on pages 26–29.

Keys for smaller groups

All the main groups can be divided into **smaller groups**. You can use a key each time.

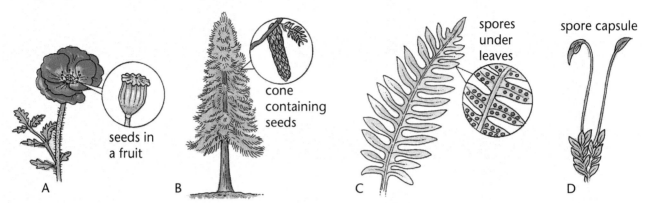

seeds in
a fruit

A

cone
containing
seeds

B

spores
under
leaves

C

spore capsule

D

3 Copy the table.

Use the key to find out which group each plant belongs to, and complete the table.

Plant	Seeds or spores?	Where seeds or spores are	Plant group
A			
B			
C			
D			

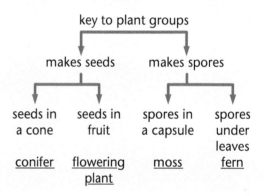

key to plant groups

makes seeds   makes spores

seeds in   seeds in   spores in   spores
a cone   fruit   a capsule   under
                                                 leaves

conifer   flowering   moss   fern
               plant

Special keys for different flowers

Each plant group can be sorted into smaller groups; for example, flowering plants.

There are too many different kinds of flowering plants for one key to cover them all.

We use separate keys for different families of flowers. For example, we can use a **key** just for flowers with four petals.

WHAT YOU NEED TO REMEMBER (Copy and complete using the **key words**)

What is it?

We can use a key to sort living things into groups and then into _____ _____.

If we want to identify flowering plants, we use a _____ which is just for them.

You need to be able to use a key to identify animals and plants.

More about classifying plants: C1.7

1.9 Sorting vertebrates

There are many different ways of sorting animals into groups. Scientists have found that some ways of doing this are more useful than others.

Some animals, like you, have bones. Scientists call these animals <u>vertebrates</u>.

We can then split up vertebrates into five smaller groups called <u>classes</u>: **fish**, **amphibians**, **reptiles**, **birds** and **mammals**.

REMEMBER from page 22

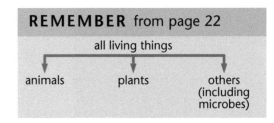

all living things

animals   plants   others (including microbes)

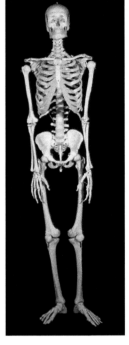

▣ Fish

1 Fish do not have lungs. How do they get the oxygen they need?

Fish get oxygen from the water through their gills.

Fish have damp scaly skins.

▣ Amphibians

2 Why do amphibians have to lay their eggs in water?

Eggs and tadpoles live in water. They would dry up on land.

Amphibians live part of their time in water and part on land.

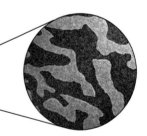

Amphibians have smooth, moist skin. They do not have scales.

▣ Reptiles

3 Write down <u>two</u> differences between amphibians and reptiles.

4 Why can reptiles lay their eggs out of water?

Reptiles have scales, but they are dry. They breathe air into their lungs.

Reptiles lay eggs on land. Their tough leathery shells stop the eggs drying out.

Birds

5 What is the difference between reptile and bird eggs?

Birds are covered with feathers. They have a beak and a pair of wings.

Birds lay eggs with hard shells. *Not all birds can fly!*

Mammals

6 Mammals have fewer young than other vertebrates because more of them survive. Why do you think this is?

Young mammals develop inside their mother's body and feed on her milk when they are born.

Mammals have hair or fur. They look after their young for a long time.

WHAT YOU NEED TO REMEMBER (Copy and complete using the **key words**)

Sorting vertebrates

Class	What it is like	Examples
_____	has scales, breathes through gills, lays eggs	cod
_____	moist smooth skin, lives on land and in water, lays eggs	frog
_____	hair covers the body, young feed on mother's milk	cat
_____	dry scaly skin, eggs have tough leathery shell	crocodile
_____	have wings, feathers cover the body, eggs have hard shell	seagull

More about classifying animals: C1.8

27

1.10 Sorting animals that don't have bones

Scientists split up animals into two main groups.

Animals that have bones are called vertebrates.

Most kinds of animals don't have bones. We call them <u>invertebrates</u>.

REMEMBER from page 22

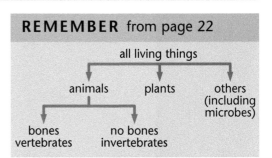

Soft-bodied invertebrates

Some invertebrates have completely soft bodies. Examples include **jellyfish**, **flatworms** and **true worms**.

A tiny jellyfish called a hydra.

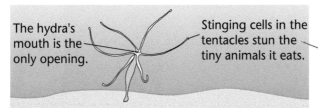

The hydra's mouth is the only opening.

Stinging cells in the tentacles stun the tiny animals it eats.

All jellyfish live in water.

1 Why should you watch out for jellyfish when you are swimming in the sea?

2 A cat or dog with a tapeworm eats a lot of food but gets thinner. Why is this?

3 Write down <u>two</u> differences between a flatworm (for example, a planarian) and a true worm.

mouth
thin, flat body, no segments

A planarian is a flatworm

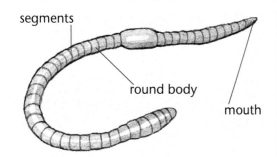

segments
round body
mouth

An earthworm is a true worm.

Ragworms are also true worms.

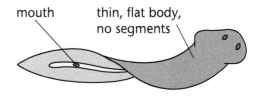

The head of a tapeworm. This kind grows to 4 metres long and lives in human intestines. It is a flatworm.

4 Copy and complete the table to show the main features of soft-bodied invertebrates.

Soft-bodied invertebrate	Main features
jellyfish	
flatworms	
true worms	

Molluscs

Other invertebrates have some hard parts.

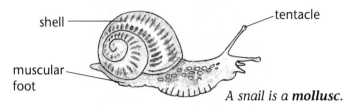

shell

tentacle

muscular foot

A snail is a **mollusc**.

The squid's shell is inside its body.

5 Most molluscs have shells. Where is a squid's shell?

The biggest group of animals on Earth!

About three-quarters of all the different kinds of animals on Earth belong to this group of invertebrates. They are called the arthropods.

There are many different kinds of arthropod, so we split them into smaller groups. But all arthropods do have some things in common:

- a hard skeleton on the outside of their bodies;
- jointed legs;

Most arthropods have feelers (antennae).

6 Look at the pictures showing different types of arthropod. Copy and complete the table.

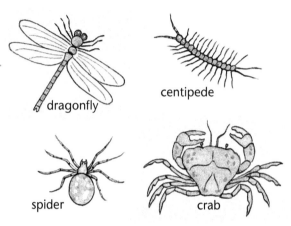

dragonfly

centipede

spider

crab

Arthropod group	What do they look like?	Examples
crustaceans	two pairs of antennae, five or more pairs of legs	
insects	three pairs of legs, one or two pairs of wings	
spiders	four pairs of legs, no antennae	
many legs	long body divided into segments, legs on every segment	

WHAT YOU NEED TO REMEMBER (Copy and complete using the **key words**)

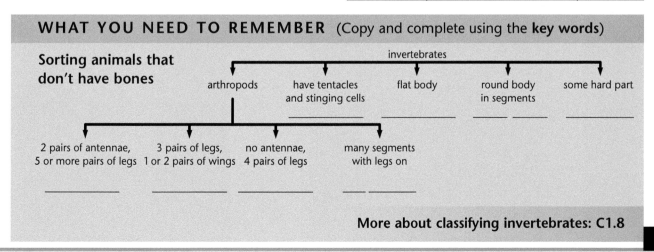

Sorting animals that don't have bones

invertebrates

arthropods | have tentacles and stinging cells | flat body | round body in segments | some hard part

2 pairs of antennae, 5 or more pairs of legs | 3 pairs of legs, 1 or 2 pairs of wings | no antennae, 4 pairs of legs | many segments with legs on

More about classifying invertebrates: C1.8

2.1 Healthy eating

Our <u>diet</u> is all the food we eat. This food has to be all the things we need, but not too much of any one thing. To stay healthy we mustn't eat too much **fat**, **sugar** or **salt**. Our food must contain **vitamins**, **minerals** and a lot of **fibre**.

■ The traffic-light diet

Here's an easy way to remember the foods to avoid (red ●) and the foods to eat plenty of (green ●).

■ ● Red – stop and think

These foods have a lot of fat or sugar or salt:

sweets, chocolate, cakes, jam, butter, cream, ice cream, fried food, fat on meat, sausages, bacon, chips and crisps.

high fat   high sugar   high salt

Some ● foods.

■ ● Amber – go carefully

Biscuits, red meat, burgers, pies, eggs, cheese, nuts, pasta, pizza, baked beans, samosas; most soft drinks.

Some ● foods.

■ ● Green – go right ahead

Fresh fruit, salad, vegetables, fish, chicken, cottage cheese, yogurt, skimmed milk, bran, bread, rice, lentils; tea (without sugar), water.

1 Name a ● food that has too much salt.

2 Why is cream a ● food?

3 Name a ● food that has a lot of fibre.

Some ● foods.

Which meal is healthier?

Working out the traffic-light colour for food can help you decide if a meal is healthy.

meal 1

meal 2

4 Copy and complete the table.

Name of food	●	●	●
Meal 1			
rice			*
chicken			
peas			
apple pie			
Meal 2			
fish fingers			
chips	*		
baked beans			
yogurt			

5 Which meal is healthier, meal 1 or meal 2?

Improving Kelly's diet

The picture shows the sort of meal Kelly usually eats.

If Kelly is not more careful all this ● food will make her unhealthy. Doctors have found a link between high fat and high salt diets and heart disease.

6 Draw a picture of a healthy meal for Kelly. Include lots of ● foods.

chocolate pudding

coffee with sugar and cream

sausages and chips

Kelly's meal.

WHAT YOU NEED TO REMEMBER (Copy and complete using the **key words**)

Healthy eating

To stay healthy we should eat plenty of _____, _____ and _____, but not too much _____, _____ and _____.

More about healthy eating: C2.3

2.2 Born to exercise

Thousands of years ago humans had to be very active just to stay alive. So all of us are born with a body ready to move about all day.

But today many people spend their time sitting down – at work, in the car or bus, and in front of the television or computer.

Thousands of years ago humans had to hunt animals for meat and search for fruits and nuts.

1 Why did people thousands of years ago have to be very active?

2 Write down <u>three</u> reasons why many people don't move about very much nowadays.

You can move about because of the muscles in your body. If you don't exercise your muscles, they won't work so well.

Many people who work in offices spend most of the day sitting down.

How to exercise your heart muscle

The most important muscle in your body is your <u>heart</u>. Your heart is a bag of muscle that squeezes blood so it moves round your body. Even when you are asleep your heart is busy pumping blood.

When you are resting, your heart beats about 70 times a minute. When you exercise, you can feel your heart beating stronger and faster. It can beat up to twice as fast as it beats at rest. This is good exercise for your heart and keeps it healthy.

3 Where is your heart?

4 About how fast does your heart beat when you exercise?

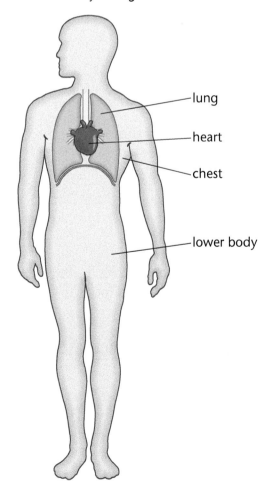

A close-up of the heart

The picture shows a person's heart during an operation.

Your heart is divided down the middle by a wall of muscle. On each side the blood is squeezed through two spaces (so that is four spaces altogether).

5 Copy and complete these sentences.

Blood comes from your body and goes into the _____ side of your heart. Your heart pumps this blood to your _____ where it gets oxygen. The blood then goes to the _____ side of your heart to be pumped around your _____ .

Your heart **pumps** blood by squeezing it out of the **ventricles**. You have **valves** in your heart. These shut when the ventricles squeeze so that blood can't go back the wrong way.

6 (a) What is there between each atrium and ventricle?

(b) What job does this do?

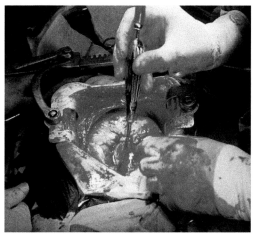

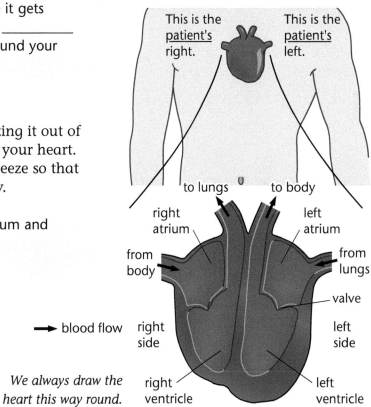

This is the patient's right.

This is the patient's left.

to lungs   to body

right atrium   left atrium

from body   from lungs

valve

→ blood flow   right side   left side

We always draw the heart this way round.   right ventricle   left ventricle

---

WHAT YOU NEED TO REMEMBER (Copy and complete using the **key words**)

Born to exercise

Your heart _____ blood to your lungs and to the rest of your body.
The _____ do this by squeezing the blood.
Your heart has _____ to stop the blood flowing the wrong way.

You need to be able to add these labels to a drawing of the heart: right* atrium, left* atrium, right* ventricle, left* ventricle, valve.   (*Remember – the person's right and left.)

More about exercise: C2.7

2.3 Where does blood travel?

Blood travels around your body in tubes. There are three kinds of tube: arteries, capillaries and veins.

Your heart pumps blood into the **arteries** which carry blood to all parts of your body.

1 Copy and complete these sentences.

Arteries split into smaller tubes called _____ that reach every part of your body. Capillaries join back together into _____ which carry blood back to your _____.

◼ Looking at arteries, capillaries and veins

The diagram shows some of the differences between arteries, capillaries and **veins**.

2 Why do arteries have thick walls?

3 Why do veins have valves?

Capillaries are very thin blood vessels all over your body. Capillary walls are very thin so that substances can move in and out of the blood easily.

4 Copy and complete this table to show what moves in and out of capillaries.

To cells	To blood
oxygen	

 Find a connection between blood, Galen, Harvey, Malpighi and a bat's wing.

REMEMBER from page 33

Your heart pumps blood around your body.

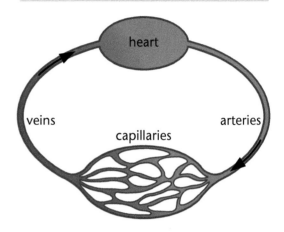

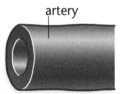

Arteries have thick strong walls because blood is at high pressure after being pumped by the heart.

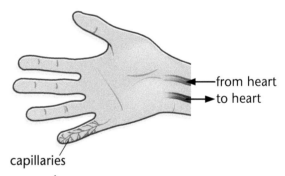

Vein walls are not very thick because the blood is at low pressure. Valves stop blood going the wrong way.

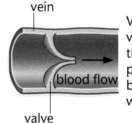

Your body is made of lots of tiny cells. No cell is far from a capillary.

Your pulse

When your heart squeezes the blood into arteries, they stretch bigger for a moment. If an artery is close to your skin, like on your wrist or neck, you can feel the artery stretching. This is your <u>pulse</u>. Each pulse you count is a heart beat.

Your pulse is faster when you exercise. More blood gets to the cells of your muscles so that they can get the things they need to work hard.

5 What <u>two</u> things does the blood carry that the muscle cells need?
(Hint: Look at the diagram at the bottom of page 34.)

How to take a pulse.

How fit are you?

You can tell how fit you are by timing how long it takes for your pulse to go back to normal after exercise. We call this your <u>recovery</u> <u>time</u>.

6 (a) Look at the graph. What is Asad's pulse rate when he is resting?

(b) How high does Asad's pulse go when he exercises?

(c) How long does it take for Asad's pulse to go back to normal after he has stopped exercising?

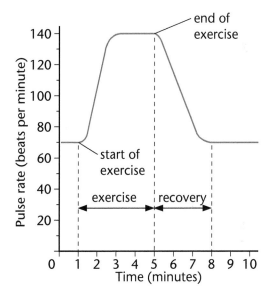

Asad's pulse rate.

WHAT YOU NEED TO REMEMBER (Copy and complete using the **key words**)

Where does blood travel?

Blood circulates around your body, from the heart to the _____ to the capillaries to the _____ and back to the heart.

Blood carries substances such as glucose and _____ to all the cells of your body.

More about keeping fit: C2.7

2.4 Your lungs

All the cells of your body need oxygen to stay alive. So you have to **breathe** air into your body. Air goes into your **lungs**.

Look at the diagram.

1 (a) How many lungs do you have?

(b) In what part of your body are they?

■ What is inside your chest

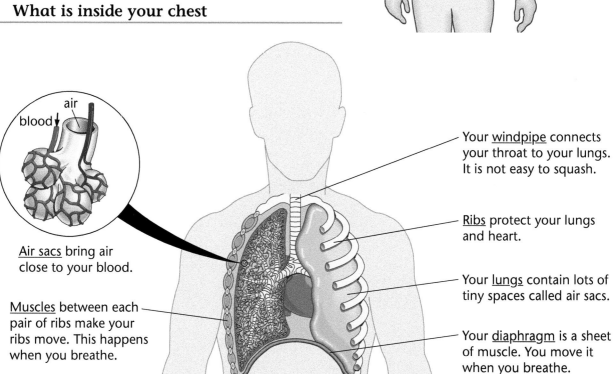

Air sacs bring air close to your blood.

Muscles between each pair of ribs make your ribs move. This happens when you breathe.

left lung

heart

chest

lower body

Your windpipe connects your throat to your lungs. It is not easy to squash.

Ribs protect your lungs and heart.

Your lungs contain lots of tiny spaces called air sacs.

Your diaphragm is a sheet of muscle. You move it when you breathe.

2 Look at the diagram. Then copy and complete the table.

Parts of your body	What jobs they do
rib muscles and diaphragm muscles	
ribs	
windpipe	
air sacs	

You say 'diaphragm' like this: 'die-a-fram'.

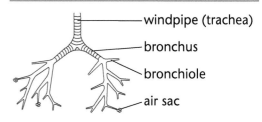

windpipe (trachea)

bronchus

bronchiole

air sac

Some people call the tubes to your lungs the bronchial tree.

◼ How you breathe

When you breathe in:

- ◼ muscles between your ribs move your ribcage up and out;

- ◼ your diaphragm moves down and becomes flatter;

- ◼ the extra space in your lungs fills with air.

When you breathe out:

- ◼ your ribs move down;

- ◼ your diaphragm curves up again;

- ◼ there is less space inside your chest so air is pushed out.

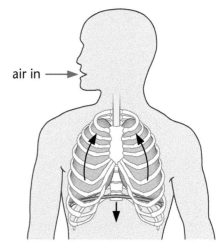

air in →

space inside your lungs:
   shallow breath 2000 cm³
   deep breath 4500 cm³

Breathing in.

3 Copy and complete the table.

	Breathing in	Breathing out
How your ribs move		
What happens to your diaphragm		

4 How much air do you breathe in:

(a) in a shallow breath;

(b) in a deep breath?

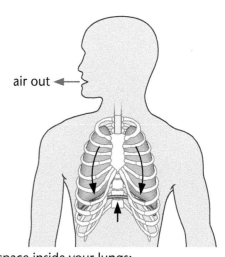

air out ←

space inside your lungs:
   1500cm³
   This means that there is 1500 cm³ of air that you can't breathe out.

Breathing out.

WHAT YOU NEED TO REMEMBER (Copy and complete using the **key words**)

Your lungs

When you _____, you take air in and out of your _____.

You need to be able to add these labels to a drawing of the breathing system: lungs, trachea (windpipe), bronchus, bronchioles, diaphragm, ribs.

More about lungs and exercise: C2.6

2.5 Breathing and asthma

Saba has asthma. This sometimes affects her lungs. It makes it difficult for her to breathe.

Saba gets wheezy when she runs on a cold day. This also happens when she breathes in smoke or pollution from cars.

1 Copy and complete these sentences.

People with asthma wheeze when the bronchioles to their lungs become _____ than normal. This makes it hard for _____ to go in and out of their _____.

The bronchioles become narrower because the lining swells. Also, muscles in the bronchiole walls contract or shorten.

> **REMEMBER** from page 36
>
> You must keep breathing air into your lungs. Then all the cells in your body can get the oxygen they need to stay alive.

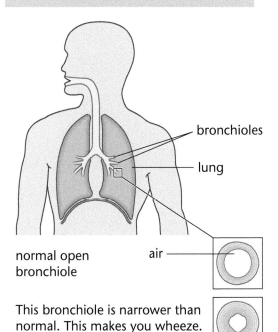

bronchioles

lung

normal open bronchiole   air

This bronchiole is narrower than normal. This makes you wheeze.

In an asthma attack, only a small hole is left for air to get in and out (like breathing through a straw).

What happens in an asthma attack.

◼ Treatment for Saba

When Saba feels her chest go tight, she uses an inhaler. She breathes in a drug from the inhaler. This drug relaxes the muscles in the walls of her bronchioles. So, the tubes widen and she can breathe more easily.

It is important that she stays calm and uses her inhaler straight away. Sometimes her breathing gets very difficult and she has an asthma attack.

2 How does an inhaler help Saba?

Using an inhaler.

A close-up of your lungs

The air you breathe in is not the same as the air you breathe out. In your lungs **oxygen** goes from the air into your blood and **carbon dioxide** goes from your blood into the air. This process is called **gas exchange**.

3 Copy and complete the table using the words <u>more</u> or <u>less</u>.

Air you breathe in	Air you breathe out
more oxygen	_____ oxygen
_____ carbon dioxide	_____ carbon dioxide

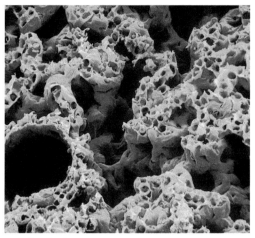

Inside the lungs are lots of tiny spaces called air sacs.

You breathe for your cells

Your blood carries the oxygen round your body. Your cells use the oxygen to get energy. Carbon dioxide is made by cells and needs to be got rid of. So your blood carries it to your lungs so that you can breathe it out.

4 When Saba has an asthma attack, what gas does she not get enough of?

5 Why does Saba feel weak when she has an asthma attack?

Our cells need more oxygen when we exercise so we breathe faster.

6 Why does Saba have more problems when she runs?

7 Saba told her new PE teacher that she had asthma. Why did she do this?

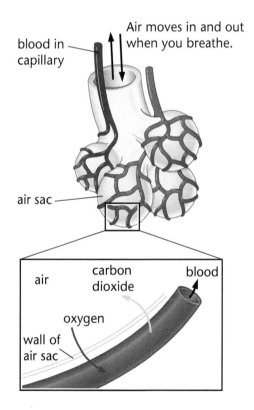

WHAT YOU NEED TO REMEMBER (Copy and complete using the **key words**)

Breathing and asthma

In your lungs, _____ passes into your blood and _____ _____ passes into the air. We call this _____ _____.

More about breathing: C2.6

39

2.6 How do we catch diseases?

Influenza

Flu (influenza) is an easy disease to catch. All you need to do is to find someone who has flu. Then let them breathe on you, or cough or sneeze near you. Tiny drops that contain microbes can travel through the air for you to breathe in. This is because the microbe that causes flu is very tiny.

1 What causes influenza?

2 Why is flu so easy to catch?

3 Why should you cough or sneeze into a tissue?

A sneeze spreads tiny drops into the air. These drops contain all sorts of microbes.

Viruses

The microbe that causes flu is a virus. There are many other **viruses**. Each type of virus causes a different disease. Some diseases are easier to catch than others. There are some diseases that you don't usually catch again after you have had them once.

4 Write down the names of <u>three</u> diseases caused by viruses.

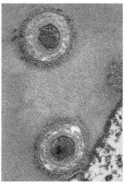 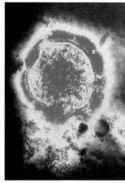

Chicken pox viruses.   *Measles virus.*
× 90,000   *× 100,000*

Bacteria

Bacteria are also microbes. Some bacteria cause disease.

5 Write down the names of <u>two</u> diseases caused by bacteria.

Microbes are tiny. These photos of viruses and bacteria are magnified enormously.

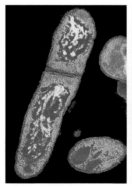 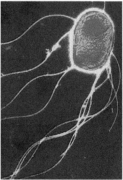

TB (tuberculosis)   *Salmonella bacterium.*
bacteria.   *It causes food*
                        poisoning.

The frozen chicken story

6 Why did the family decide it was the chicken that caused the food poisoning?

7 What sort of microbe is salmonella?

Salmonella bacteria are often found in chickens. To kill salmonella bacteria, you must make them very hot. We need to see inside the chicken to find out what went wrong.

8 Does freezing kill salmonella?

9 What should the boys have done to cook the chicken properly?

chicken after defrosting for 1 hour

still frozen

chicken after cooking for 2 hours

cooked, hot (bacteria killed)

not cooked, only warm (bacteria not killed)

WHAT YOU NEED TO REMEMBER (Copy and complete using the **key words**)

How do we catch diseases?

Some bacteria and viruses can make you ill. Different microbes cause different diseases.
For example, _____ cause tuberculosis (TB) and salmonella food poisoning.
_____ cause influenza and chicken pox.

More about illness: C2.1

2.7 Harmful chemicals

There are lots of different chemicals that can **harm** you. Examples are tobacco smoke and alcohol. But many people still choose to take these into their bodies.

■ Smoking

Nicotine in **tobacco** smoke stops the tiny hairs in your lungs from working. It also increases your heart rate. The tar in cigarette smoke can cause cancer.

1 Write down <u>two</u> ways nicotine damages your body.

2 What other dangerous substance is there in cigarette smoke?

■ Drinking alcohol

Alcohol is a drug that changes the way you behave and move. When you drink, your reactions slow down. People who are drunk slur their words and become clumsy. Over a long time alcohol can damage your liver and your brain.

3 Why is it dangerous to drink and drive?

4 Which <u>two</u> organs of the body does alcohol damage?

■ Solvent abuse

This is when people breathe in the fumes from some sort of glue or other substances containing solvents. The effects are similar to being drunk. But these fumes can make your heart stop or make you choke to death.

5 Describe <u>three</u> ways you can tell if someone has been glue sniffing.

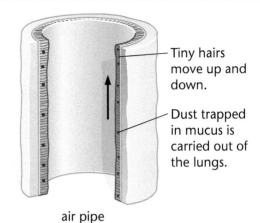

Tiny hairs move up and down.

Dust trapped in mucus is carried out of the lungs.

air pipe

Nicotine in tobacco smoke paralyses the tiny hairs which clean dust out of your lungs. So smokers' lungs get dusty. This is why they cough.

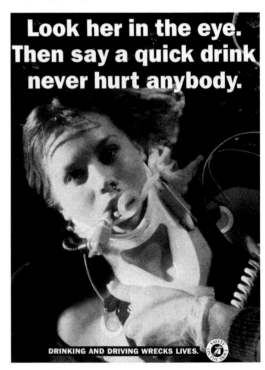

Look her in the eye. Then say a quick drink never hurt anybody.

DRINKING AND DRIVING WRECKS LIVES.

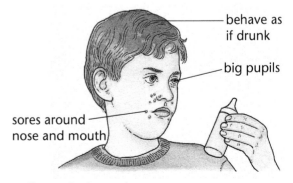

behave as if drunk

big pupils

sores around nose and mouth

Signs of solvent abuse.

▪ Illegal drugs

People caught with illegal drugs could spend up to 7 years in prison.

<u>LSD (Acid)</u> affects your mind. People who take it see strange things and can feel upset and depressed. This can happen without warning even several years after it is taken.

6 Why is LSD a dangerous drug?

<u>Ecstasy</u> makes your heart beat faster than normal. People use this at raves to help them dance for hours. They get hot and sweat a lot. They need to replace the water and salts they lose. If they don't they can die of heat stroke. Too much water can also kill them.

7 Why do you think some people who take Ecstasy have overheated?

There's only one truth about Ecstasy: it kills

<u>Cannabis</u> is usually smoked and it can cause mouth and throat cancer. People who smoke cannabis feel relaxed.

8 What illness do tobacco and cannabis both cause?

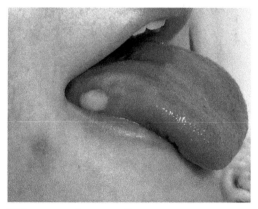

This person has mouth cancer.

WHAT YOU NEED TO REMEMBER (Copy and complete using the **key words**)

Harmful chemicals

Drugs can _____ you. They affect your mind and body.
Even legal drugs like _____ and _____ are harmful.

More about harmful chemicals: C2.2

2.8 Long-term effects of drugs

Addiction

An <u>addict</u> is a person who can't manage without something.

Heroin and cocaine are addictive drugs. So are **nicotine** and **alcohol**. If you stop using them you feel ill. This is why once people start smoking or drinking a lot of alcohol they find it hard to stop.

A lot of ordinary people are addicted to smoking cigarettes or to alcohol. Over the years their bodies will be damaged.

1 Do you think the people in the picture are addicts? Give reasons for your answer.

Lung cancer

Look at the graph.

2 **(a)** How many people (in 10 000) who don't smoke die of lung cancer?

(b) How many people (in 10 000) who smoke 40 cigarettes a day die of lung cancer?

Half the people who have operations to remove lung cancer continue to smoke.

3 Why do you think people who have been made ill by smoking continue to smoke?

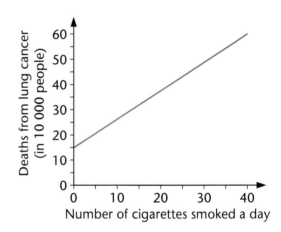

■ Other effects of drugs

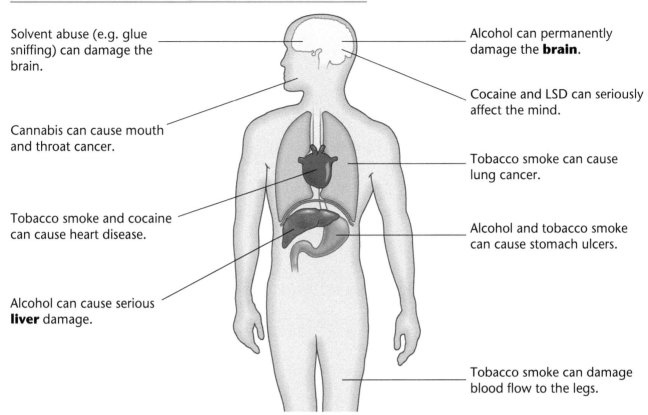

Solvent abuse (e.g. glue sniffing) can damage the brain.

Cannabis can cause mouth and throat cancer.

Tobacco smoke and cocaine can cause heart disease.

Alcohol can cause serious **liver** damage.

Alcohol can permanently damage the **brain**.

Cocaine and LSD can seriously affect the mind.

Tobacco smoke can cause lung cancer.

Alcohol and tobacco smoke can cause stomach ulcers.

Tobacco smoke can damage blood flow to the legs.

4 Which parts of the body does alcohol damage?

5 Copy and complete this table to show how drugs can damage your body.

Effect on the body	Drugs
brain damage	
heart disease and blood flow problems	
lung cancer	
liver damage	
stomach ulcers	

WHAT YOU NEED TO REMEMBER (Copy and complete using the **key words**)

Long-term effects of drugs

You can become addicted to _____, _____ and other drugs.

Drugs can damage your body.
For example, alcohol damages your _____ and your _____.

More about drugs: C2.2

2.9 Your skeleton

You have a skeleton inside your body. It is made of lots of bones all joined together.

Your skeleton holds your body together in the right shape. We say it <u>supports</u> your body.

Your skeleton **protects** some of the softer parts of your body.

You need a skeleton to move about. Bones give **muscles** something to pull on.

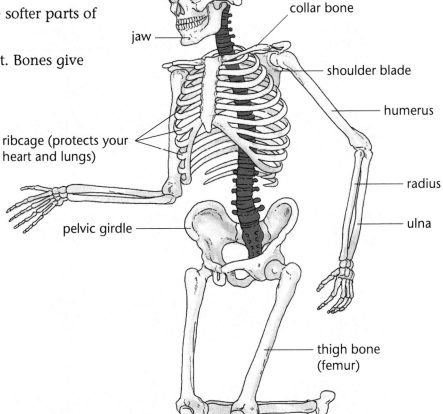

skull (protects your brain)

collar bone

jaw

shoulder blade

humerus

ribcage (protects your heart and lungs)

radius

ulna

pelvic girdle

thigh bone (femur)

knee cap

shin bone (tibia)

fibula

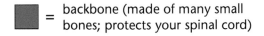 = backbone (made of many small bones; protects your spinal cord)

1 What is a skeleton?

2 Write down <u>three</u> jobs your skeleton does.

3 Look at the diagram. Then copy and complete the table.

Bone	What it protects
ribcage	
	brain
backbone	

■ Broken bones

Bones are strong but they can break.

Sumera fell off her bike and landed on her arm. At the hospital the doctors X-ray her arm to see which bones are broken.

4 Which bones has Sumera broken?

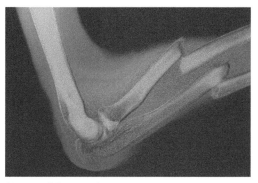

X-ray of Sumera's arm.

A broken bone will not heal straight unless the broken ends are held in position.

Bones support your body. If a bone is broken it will not support you.

5 Write down <u>two</u> reasons why Sumera must wear a cast on her broken arm.

 Röntgen discovered X-rays in 1895. Soon they were used for looking at bones and then other organs in the body. Find out <u>two</u> other uses of X-rays.

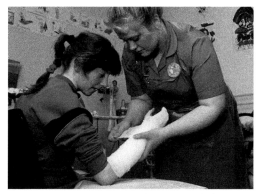

Sumera wears a cast on her arm while the bone mends.

■ Marrow bones

Some bones have a soft **marrow** inside them. Bone marrow makes new blood cells.

6 Look at the diagram. How can bones be light and strong at the same time?

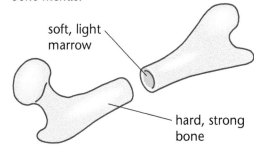

soft, light marrow

hard, strong bone

A tube of bone is a lot lighter than solid bone. It is still very strong.

WHAT YOU NEED TO REMEMBER (Copy and complete using the **key words**)

Your skeleton

■ supports your body;

■ _____ organs like your brain;

Your bones:

■ give _____ something to pull on;

■ have bone _____ to make new blood cells.

You need to be able to label a drawing of the main parts of your skeleton.

More about bones and muscles: C2.8

2.10 Joints

REMEMBER from page 46

Your skeleton is made of lots of bones joined together.

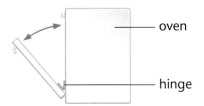

The hinge of an oven door only bends one way, like your elbow joint.

The places where your bones are joined together are called **joints**. Muscles are fixed to your bones on each side of a joint. Your muscles pull on the bones to make you move.

■ Elbow joint

In your elbow the bones fit together so the joint only bends one way. This is like a hinge.

To bend your arm, your biceps muscle shortens or **contracts**. This pulls one bone towards the other.

To straighten your arm, your biceps muscle relaxes and the muscle on the other side of the joint contracts. This pulls the arm straight again.

1 Look at the diagram. Then copy and complete the table.

	Arm straight	Arm bent
Contracting muscle		
Relaxing muscle		

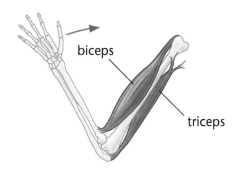

The biceps contracts to bend the arm. The triceps relaxes to let this happen.

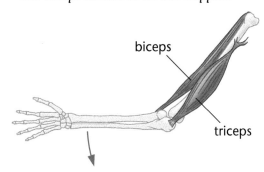

The triceps contracts to straighten the arm. The biceps relaxes to let this happen.

■ Hip joint

The end of your thigh bone is round like a ball. It fits into a hollow called a socket. This socket is part of your pelvic girdle. We call this joint a <u>ball and socket</u> joint.

2 (a) Which bone of your hip joint is the ball?

(b) Which bone of your hip joint is the socket?

(c) Which way can your hip joint bend?

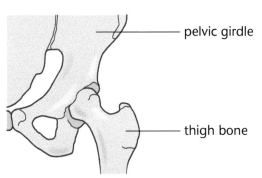

Your hip joint is a ball and socket joint. It can bend in any direction.

Backbone joint

The joints in your backbone hold the bones so they cannot move very much. Inside your backbone is your spinal cord.

3 Why mustn't the bones of your backbone move very much?

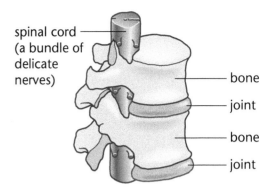

The bones of your backbone protect your spinal cord.

Replacing a joint

Marcia's grandfather Jack has had a hip replacement operation. Before the operation he had trouble walking. His hip caused him so much pain he had to stop every few steps. In Jack's hip joint the bones didn't move smoothly against each other, they rubbed and caused pain.

In the hip replacement operation, the joint between Jack's hip bone and leg bone was cut out. Then a plastic and metal joint was put in.

4 (a) What is the ball of the new joint made of?

(b) What is the socket of the new joint made of?

5 How will a hip replacement improve Jack's life?

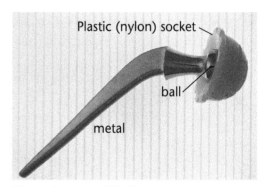

The replacement hip joint.

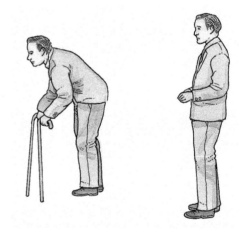

Jack before and after the operation.

WHAT YOU NEED TO REMEMBER (Copy and complete using the **key words**)

Joints

Bones let you move. Places where two bones meet are called _____.
When a muscle _____, it pulls on a bone and moves it.

More about joints: C2.8

3.1 Fuel and energy

We burn fuel to give us energy.

1 Write down <u>two</u> things we use this energy for.

2 Write down the names of <u>two</u> fuels that we burn.

Burning gas gives us heat for cooking.

Burning petrol makes things move.

All plants and animals also need energy. They get this from **food**. Food is their fuel.

3 Humans are animals. Write down <u>three</u> things we use energy for.

 **moving**  **growing**

 keeping warm

Different plants and animals need different amounts of food for energy.

What we use energy for.

4 (a) For each pair of pictures, copy and complete the sentence.

The _____ bee needs more energy than the _____ bee.

The _____ needs more energy than the _____.

(b) Give reasons for your answers to (a).

Briton   Inuit

Resting    Flying

Releasing energy from fuels

fuel

oxygen

→ energy

food

oxygen

→ energy

5 Copy and complete the sentence.

Cars and humans need to take in _____ to release energy from _____.

Which foods give us energy?

Some of the substances in our food give us energy. These are mainly <u>carbohydrates</u> and <u>fats</u>.

> We measure energy in joules (J) or kilojoules (kJ). 1000 joules make 1 kilojoule.

6 Look at the burger.

(a) How much energy does it give you?

(b) Which part of the burger provides most of this energy?

bread (mainly carbohydrate) 650 kJ

chicken (mainly protein) 580 kJ

butter (mainly fat) 150 kJ

Why do we need proteins?

7 Look at the diagram, then copy and complete the sentences.

We use proteins mainly for _____ and _____. But if we eat more protein than we need for growing new _____, we use what is left for _____.

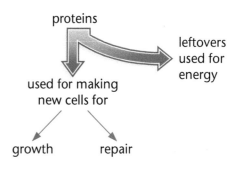

proteins

used for making new cells for

growth   repair

leftovers used for energy

WHAT YOU NEED TO REMEMBER (Copy and complete using the **key words**)

Fuel and energy

We need energy for _____, _____ and keeping warm.
We get this energy from _____. Food is our fuel.

More about food and energy: C3.4

51

3.2 Food for humans

■ Living off the land

If someone is 'living off the land', it means that they catch animals and collect wild plants for food.

Soldiers learn to do this as part of their training. It is called survival training.

All humans used to get their food this way. Some people still do.

1 Write down <u>three</u> things a person living off the land might eat.

2 People who gather food like this usually need to move from place to place. Why is this?

This fish is a trout.

Blackberries often grow in hedgerows.

The meat from a deer is called venison.

■ Farming the land

People living off the land found it hard to find food in the winter. They started to grow food crops like wheat during the summer and saved some for the winter.

They also started to keep animals like sheep and cattle for meat and milk.

3 Copy and complete the sentences.

Farmers may have found it easier to survive the _____ than people who hunted for food because they _____ food.

When we turn milk into cheese, we can keep it for a long time.

We can store dried grain.

Food in Britain today

Most of us don't grow our own food. A small number of farmers grow it for everybody. Even farmers in other countries grow some of our food.

All of our food comes from **plants** and **animals**. However, it is often hard to tell which ones it came from. This is because it is changed before we get it.

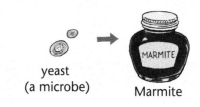

wheat   flour   bread

4 Copy and complete the sentences.

We make bread from _____ which comes from _____.

We make cheese from _____ which comes from _____.

Marmite is made from a microbe called _____.

cow   milk   cheese

Wherever it comes from, our food gives us:

- the **energy** we need to live;
- the **materials** we need to grow and to repair damaged parts.

yeast
(a microbe)   Marmite

How does the energy get into food?

Look at the picture.

5 Copy and complete the diagram.

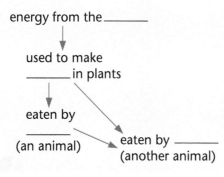

energy from the _____

↓

used to make _____ in plants

↓

eaten by _____
(an animal)

eaten by _____
(another animal)

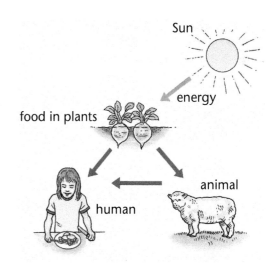

Sun

energy

food in plants

human

animal

WHAT YOU NEED TO REMEMBER (Copy and complete using the **key words**)

Food for humans

Our food gives us the _____ and the _____ we need to live and to grow. It comes from _____ or from _____ which ate plants.

More about food and energy: C3.4

3.3 What most of your food is made of

If you eat more food than you need, you store it as fat. If you don't eat enough food, you lose weight and become weak and ill.

It also matters what type of food you eat.

Your <u>diet</u> is everything you eat. You must include carbohydrate, fat, protein and fibre in your diet. Your body needs all of these to keep **healthy**.

> **REMEMBER** from page 50
>
> Food is fuel. It gives you energy. You need food for moving about, keeping warm and growing.

These wrestlers wanted to get fat so they ate too much food.

Some people can't get enough food.

■ Energy foods

Carbohydrates and **fats** in your food give you most of your energy.

1 Write down the names of <u>two</u> sorts of food which contain a lot of carbohydrates.

2 Write down the names of <u>two</u> foods which contain a lot of fat.

Eating too much of the foods that give you energy can make you overweight. Being overweight can put a strain on your heart.

3 Write down the names of <u>two</u> sorts of food you should eat less of if you want to lose weight.

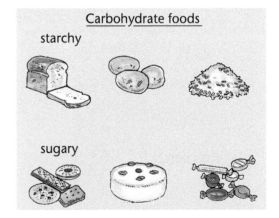

Carbohydrate foods

starchy

sugary

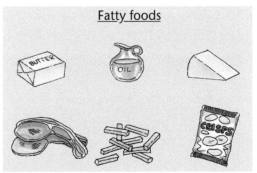

Fatty foods

These foods give us energy.

Growth foods

Your body needs **proteins** and some fat to make new cells and repair damaged ones.
Young people need lots of proteins because they are still growing.

4 Write down the names of <u>two</u> foods which contain a lot of protein.

5 Why do children need to eat more protein than adults?

6 What else besides protein do you need to make new cells?

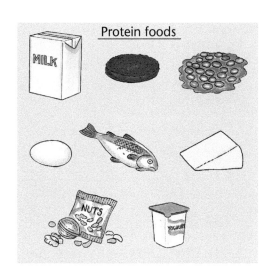

Protein foods

Food to keep you regular

When you eat food, the muscles of your intestines push the food along. **Fibre** is the part of food that you cannot digest. It gives the muscles of your intestines something to push on.

7 Write down <u>two</u> foods that could help someone who was constipated to go to the toilet.

Fibrous foods

Water

The food we eat contains a lot of water. We also need to drink **water**. Water is important to keep blood flowing and cells working.

8 What percentage of an apple is water?

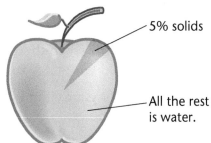

5% solids

All the rest is water.

An apple may not look like a drink, but most of it is water.

WHAT YOU NEED TO REMEMBER (Copy and complete using the **key words**)

What most of your food is made of

You need the right amount and types of food to stay _____.
You also need to drink _____.

Most food is made of _____, _____, _____, _____ and _____.

More about healthy food: C2.3

3.4 What else must there be in your food?

Adults often say to children: 'Eat your greens. They are good for you.' Have you ever thought why?

Green vegetables contain special substances called **vitamins** that you need to keep you healthy.

Illness caused by an unhealthy diet

Scurvy is a serious disease. Your gums bleed, your teeth become loose and your muscles get weak. Many years ago, sailors on long sea voyages used to get scurvy and some even died.

1 Write down <u>two</u> things that happen to you if you get scurvy.

In 1747, Dr James Lind tried an experiment on 12 men with scurvy. The table shows what happened.

2 What do you think Dr Lind told sailors to do about scurvy?

People get scurvy when there is not enough of a chemical called <u>vitamin C</u> in their diet.

You get most of your vitamin C from eating fresh fruit and vegetables.

3 Why did the men with scurvy who drank cider get a bit better?

As well as vitamin C, you need other vitamins to stay healthy. You also need **minerals** such as iron and calcium.

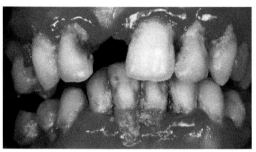

Scurvy causes bleeding gums.

What Dr Lind gave the men every day	What happened
oranges and lemons	The men got better.
cider (made from apples)	The men got a bit better.
other foods, but no fresh fruit or vegetables	The men didn't get better.

These foods contain vitamin C.

Food for health

Most foods have some vitamins or minerals, but some foods (like most sweets) don't have any.

Each type of vitamin or mineral is needed for a particular job. Each one is important for a healthy body.

Vitamin or mineral	What it is needed for
A	helps you see in dim light, and keeps your lungs healthy
B	helps many of the chemical reactions in your body
C	keeps your skin and gums healthy
D	helps you take in the minerals you need to make bones
iron	makes red blood cells
calcium	for strong bones and teeth

4 Which vitamin do you need to help you see well in dim light?

5 Write down the names of <u>two</u> foods which contain vitamin B.

6 Which mineral do you need for strong teeth?

7 In sunlight you can make vitamin D in your skin, but you still need some from your food. Write down <u>two</u> foods that contain vitamin D.

8 Meena has been told by her doctor to take some iron tablets. What does she need them for?

 Find out the connections between vitamins and Christiaan Eijkmann, Joseph Goldberger and Linus Pauling.

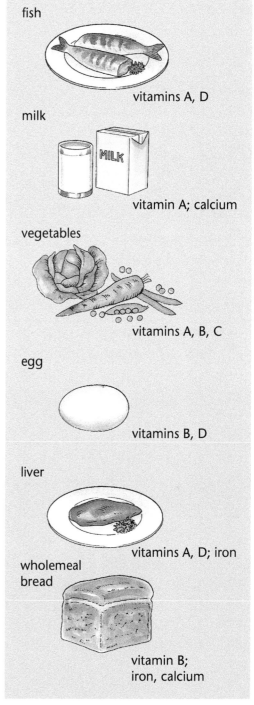

fish — vitamins A, D

milk — vitamin A; calcium

vegetables — vitamins A, B, C

egg — vitamins B, D

liver — vitamins A, D; iron

wholemeal bread — vitamin B; iron, calcium

Examples of vitamins and minerals in different foods.

WHAT YOU NEED TO REMEMBER (Copy and complete using the **key words**)

What else must there be in your food?

To stay healthy you need to eat foods that contain _____ and _____.

More about healthy food: C2.3

3.5 Where does your food go?

When you swallow your food, it is starting on a long journey. This can last for several days.

Cutting food up

You can put a large piece of food in your mouth. It is easier to swallow smaller pieces, so you use your teeth to cut and chew the food.

1 What happens if you try to swallow a very large piece of food?

2 Why is important to take good care of your teeth?

Salivary glands make the saliva in your mouth. Saliva is a digestive juice. It also makes your food slippery and easy to swallow.

Once swallowed, muscles in your oesophagus (gullet) push the food into your stomach.

3 Copy and complete these sentences.

Your _____ cut and chew your food.
Saliva wets food so it is easier to _____.

What happens after you swallow?

The photographs on this page are of a person who has had a special drink. The drink shows up on X-ray photographs so we can see where food goes.

4 List in order the parts that your food goes through after you swallow.

These parts, and the glands that make digestive juices, work together. They are your <u>digestive system</u>.

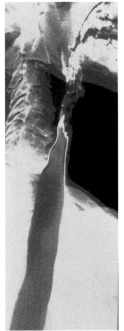 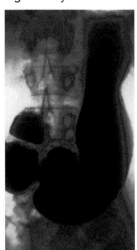

X-ray photographs of a liquid passing through a person's digestive system.

Oesophagus (gullet). Stomach.

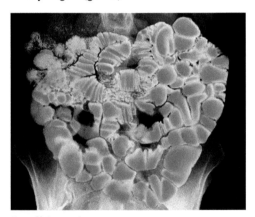

Small intestine.

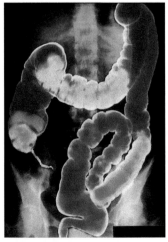

Large intestine.

In your stomach

Muscles in the stomach wall churn the food up. Glands in the stomach lining add more digestive juices.

Food can stay in your stomach for 3–4 hours. Liquids leave sooner. Your stomach lets food out a bit at a time into the small intestine.

5 Copy and complete the table.

Part of stomach	What it does
muscles in wall	
glands in lining	
ring of muscle	

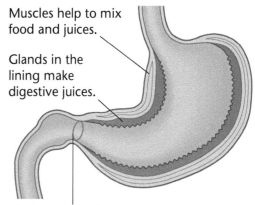

Muscles help to mix food and juices.

Glands in the lining make digestive juices.

A ring of muscle controls what leaves the stomach.

DID YOU KNOW?

There are about 6 metres of intestines inside your body.

In the intestines

6 Look at the diagram opposite. How do all your intestines fit into the lower part of your body?

In the small intestines, more digestive juices are added to your food.

7 What <u>two</u> parts of your body add digestive juices to the food in your small intestine?

Digested food passes into your blood from your small intestine. Blood carries the food to cells that need it.

Your food and drinks also contain a lot of water. Water passes into your blood from the large intestine.

The food that is left contains undigested waste, water and bacteria. We call this waste <u>faeces</u>. This passes through the large intestine and eventually leaves your body.

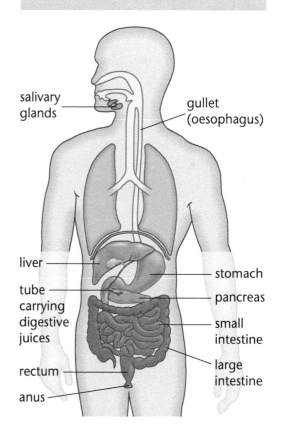

salivary glands

gullet (oesophagus)

liver

tube carrying digestive juices

rectum

anus

stomach

pancreas

small intestine

large intestine

WHAT YOU NEED TO REMEMBER

Where does your food go?

You must be able to label a diagram of the digestive system like the one above.

More about digestion: C2.4

3.6 Digesting your food

Food contains large molecules which you cannot absorb into your blood. You need to break these down. Your digestive system does this.

You can't, like the snake, swallow a whole rat, but you still eat your food in large pieces.

What happens during digestion?

You put a large piece of food in your mouth.

Chewing your food cuts it into smaller pieces.

But even a small piece of food has large molecules in it.

Parts of the digestive system make digestive juices. The juices contain enzymes which break down large food molecules into **smaller** ones. This is **digestion**.

The chemical links in the molecule are broken. Different types of food are broken down like this:

- carbohydrates → glucose;

- fats → fatty acids and glycerol;

- proteins → amino acids.

1 What is digestion?

2 Copy and complete these sentences.

Your teeth cut food into _____ pieces. Even these small pieces can have large _____ in them.

To make the molecules smaller, _____ _____ are added to the food. These break the _____ links in the large food molecules.

The _____ molecules are broken down into _____ ones. Small molecules are soluble. This means that they can dissolve.

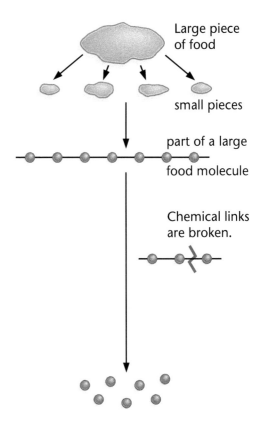

Large piece of food

small pieces

part of a large food molecule

Chemical links are broken.

■ What happens to the digested food?

All the cells in your body need food.

Digested food passes into the **blood** from the small intestines. This is **absorption**. Only small soluble molecules are absorbed.

3 (a) Write down four substances that you can absorb from your small intestine.

(b) Where does food go when it is absorbed?

4 Write down two reasons why large food molecules must be digested.

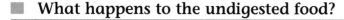

large food molecule in small intestine

blood

digestion

blood

Small, soluble food molecules are absorbed into the blood.

■ What happens to the undigested food?

The food that is left contains undigested waste, water and bacteria. We call this solid waste faeces.

The waste leaves your body through the anus. We say that the waste is egested.

The undigested waste in your faeces is mainly fibre. The muscles in your intestine walls push on fibre to move food along.

5 If you don't eat enough fibre you can become constipated. Why do you think this is?

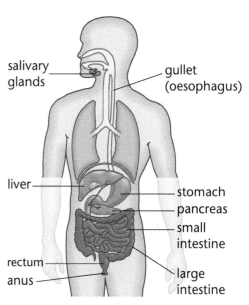

salivary glands

gullet (oesophagus)

liver

stomach

pancreas

small intestine

rectum

anus

large intestine

■ The complete story of digestion

6 These sentences are in the wrong order. They explain what happens to food in your digestive system. Copy them out in the correct order.

■ More digestive juices are added in the small intestine.
■ Solid waste leaves the body through the anus.
■ Food is chewed and saliva is added.
■ In the large intestine water passes into the blood.
■ Digested food passes into the blood here too.
■ Glands in the stomach add more digestive juices.

WHAT YOU NEED TO REMEMBER (Copy and complete using the **key words**)

Digesting your food

In your digestive system, you break large food molecules down into _____, soluble molecules. This is called _____.

These small molecules can pass into your _____. This is called _____.

More about digestion: C2.4

3.7 Absorbing and using food

REMEMBER from page 60

Your digestive system breaks food down into molecules which are small enough to absorb.

You absorb into your **blood**:

- glucose;
- fatty acids and glycerol;
- amino acids;
- vitamins;
- minerals;
- water.

Your blood takes food substances to all your **cells**.

1 Look at the diagram, then copy and complete the sentences.

You _____ food from your _____ system into your blood. Blood _____ it to all parts of your body. It goes into the _____ which need it.

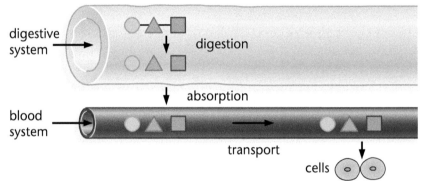

Why do your cells need food?

Your food gives your cells the **energy** and the **materials** they need to live and grow.

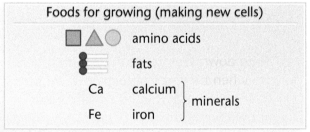

Foods to keep your cells working

water   vitamins   minerals

2 Look at the diagrams, then copy and complete the table.

Food for energy	Food for making new cells

3 Write a list of the foods your cells need to help them to work properly.

■ How do your cells get energy from food?

You take oxygen into your body in your lungs. Like your food, it travels to your cells in your blood.

REMEMBER from page 51

You need oxygen to release energy from fuels such as food.

4 Copy and complete this diagram to show the journey of oxygen.

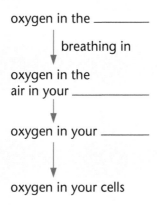

oxygen in the _____

↓ breathing in

oxygen in the air in your _____

↓

oxygen in your _____

↓

oxygen in your cells

In your cells, glucose and oxygen react together to release energy. We say that your cells **respire**.

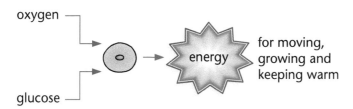

oxygen ─┐
        └→ ● → energy → for moving, growing and keeping warm
glucose ─┘

5 Write down the names of <u>two</u> substances your cells use when they respire.

6 Write down <u>three</u> things your cells need energy for.

oxygen in the air

You breathe air in.

lungs

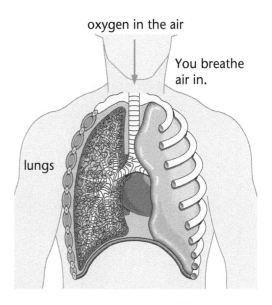

<u>In your lungs</u>   Dissolved oxygen goes into your blood.

blood →

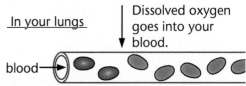

<u>Everywhere in your body</u>

blood →

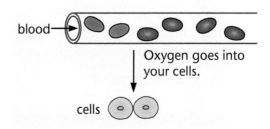

Oxygen goes into your cells.

cells

WHAT YOU NEED TO REMEMBER (Copy and complete using the **key words**)

Absorbing and using food

Your _____ transports small molecules of food to your _____.

Your cells use some of these molecules, together with oxygen, to give them _____.
We say they _____.

Your food also gives cells the _____ they need to grow.

More about using food: C2.5

3.8 How do plants grow?

New plants often come from seeds. Plants store food in their seeds. But there isn't enough food in a sunflower seed for it to grow into such a big plant.

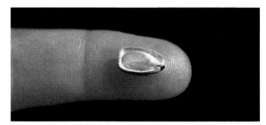

Sunflower plants grow from a seed like this.

1 In the picture, Jenny is 120 cm tall. How tall is the tallest sunflower plant?

How a seed starts to grow

Jenny planted some seeds in warm, damp soil. They took in water and started to grow. They do this only when conditions are just right.

Look at the pictures.

2 Which part of the seedling grows first?

Like you, plants need food such as glucose and proteins for energy and for growing. The seedling uses stored food from the seed. It also gets bigger because of the water it takes in. The root **hairs** absorb most of this water.

3 Write down <u>one</u> reason why root hairs are important.

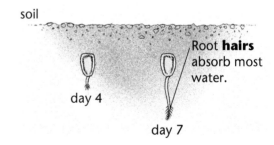

soil

Root **hairs** absorb most water.

day 4

day 7

Soon a shoot starts to grow

4 On which day did the shoot start to come up out of the ground?

The plant has now used up most of the stored food. To keep on growing it needs some way of getting more food.

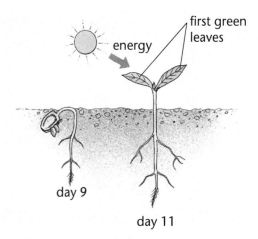

Making food to grow more

Unlike you, a plant can make food. It makes most of its food in its leaves.

Light makes the leaves turn green. The green substance in leaves is called <u>chlorophyll</u>. This traps light energy for making food.

Plants also use **water** and **carbon dioxide** to make food.

5 On which day did the sunflower start to make food? Give a reason for your answer.

6 Look at the diagram, then copy and complete the table.

What a plant needs to make food	Where it comes from
water	
carbon dioxide	
light	

When plants make food, we call it **photosynthesis**.

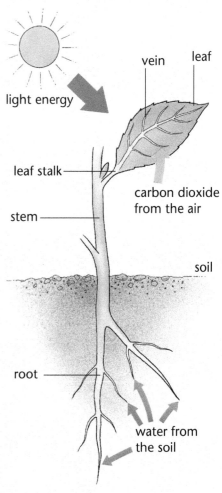

WHAT YOU NEED TO REMEMBER (Copy and complete using the **key words**)

How do plants grow?

Leaves use energy from sunlight, _____ _____ and _____ to make food. We call this process _____.

Root _____ take in water.   **More about photosynthesis: C3.2**

3.9 Minerals for plant growth

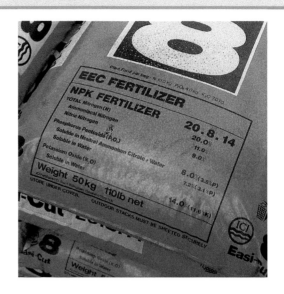

Plants use carbon dioxide and water to make their own food. But plants need other chemicals too.

Some people say that they 'feed' their plants. They mean that they give them fertilisers. Fertilisers contain the **minerals** the plants need.

1 Look at the fertiliser label. Write down the three main minerals plants get from this fertiliser.

These minerals contain chemical **elements** that plants need to grow.

2 Look at the table, then copy and complete the sentences.

Nitrates contain the element _____.
Phosphates contain the _____ phosphorus.
_____ is an element.

Element	Mineral
nitrogen (N)	nitrate
phosphorus (P)	phosphate
potassium (K)	potassium salt

■ What happens if plants don't get minerals?

To find out what happens if plants don't get these minerals, we can grow them in water or clean sand. We can then add different minerals to see how well they grow.

3 Why do we grow the plants in clean sand or water instead of soil in this experiment?

Apart from giving them different minerals, we need to grow the plants in <u>identical conditions</u>.

4 (a) Why must we grow the plants in identical conditions?

(b) Write down <u>three</u> things which need to be the same.

At the start of the experiment the plants are very similar. We make sure that all the plants get the same amount of water, heat and light.

An example – nitrates

Look at the pictures.

5 (a) Write down <u>two</u> differences between plants A and B.

(b) Write down what these differences tell us about plants and nitrates.

A This plant has all the minerals it needs.

B This plant didn't get any nitrates.

What do plants use nitrates for?

Look at the diagram.

6 Copy and complete the sentences.

Like you, plants need proteins for _____.
They need _____ and minerals such as
_____ for making these proteins.

7 Explain, as fully as you can, why you think plants A and B are different.

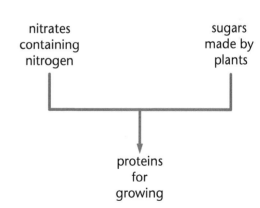

WHAT YOU NEED TO REMEMBER (Copy and complete using the **key words**)

Minerals for plant growth

Plants need chemical _____ such as nitrogen for growth.
They take them in as _____ such as nitrates.

More about minerals: C3.3

3.10 How plants take in what they need

■ Leaves take in sunlight and carbon dioxide

Leaves are **thin** and **flat**.

They are only a few cells thick so that light and carbon dioxide can reach the cells inside.

1 Copy and complete the sentences.

Leaves look green because their cells contain lots of tiny _____.
These have a green substance called _____ inside them.

2 Where does a plant take in carbon dioxide?

> **REMEMBER** from page 65
>
> To make **food**, plants need:
> ■ sunlight;
> ■ water and minerals;
> ■ carbon dioxide.

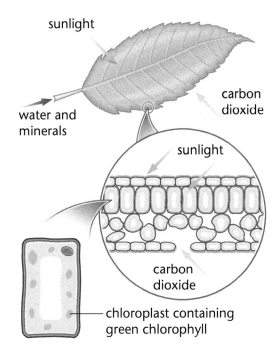

sunlight

carbon dioxide

water and minerals

sunlight

carbon dioxide

chloroplast containing green chlorophyll

■ Roots take in water and minerals

Roots take in the minerals and the water which plants need. Most of these go in through the **root hairs**. We say root hairs <u>absorb</u> them.

3 Look at the drawing. Describe, as fully as you can, where the root hairs are.

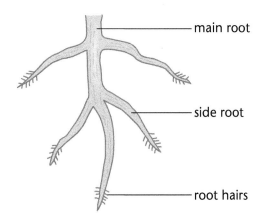

main root

side root

root hairs

Where do the water and minerals go?

Look at the diagram.

4 Copy and complete the sentences.

Root hairs take in _____ and _____.
The water and minerals then pass into special
tubes. These tubes are long and very thin, and go
from the roots to the _____ and all the way
up to the _____. They are made of many
_____.

tube of many cells
for carrying water
and minerals

to leaves

to stem

root hair

grain
of soil

soil water
containing
minerals

Arrows show
where the water and minerals go.

What else do roots do?

Plant roots are not just for taking in water and
minerals. They have another job too.

Roots hold plants in the soil so that they don't
come out of the soil easily. We say they **anchor**
plants so that they don't get uprooted.

5 Write down <u>two</u> things which could uproot a plant.

The wind uprooted this tree.

A badger dug up these bluebell bulbs.

WHAT YOU NEED TO REMEMBER (Copy and complete using the **key words**)

How plants take in what they need

Plant leaves make _____.

Leaves which are _____ and _____ are best for taking in the sunlight and
carbon dioxide the plant needs.

The water and minerals a plant needs go into it through its _____ _____.
They pass in special tubes through the root and stem to the leaves.

Roots also _____ plants in the soil.

More about minerals: C3.3

4.1 Making babies

To make a baby we need two special cells. They are called <u>sex cells</u>. One of these cells comes from the father. The other comes from the mother.

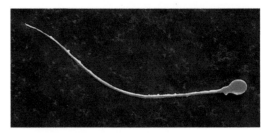

A male sex cell. This is called a sperm.

1 What are the mother's sex cells called?

2 What are the father's sex cells called?

3 Why do humans make sex cells?

> We say: one ovum
> two ova

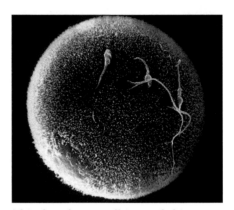

*This female sex cell is much bigger than the male sex cells around it. Female sex cells are called eggs or **ova**.*

Where sex cells are made

Sex cells are made in special places in your body. Making babies is called <u>reproduction</u>. So we call the places where sex cells are made the <u>reproductive organs</u>.

A woman has two **ovaries** that make the eggs. She also has a **uterus** (also called a womb) inside which a baby can grow.

A man has two **testes** where **sperm** are made. He also has a **penis**.

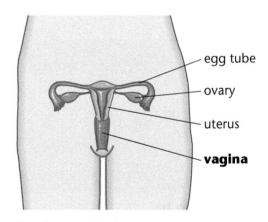

Female reproductive organs.

4 Copy and complete the sentences

Ova (eggs) are made in a woman's _____.
Sperm are made in a man's _____.

> We say: one testis
> two testes

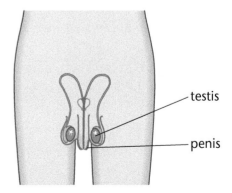

Male reproductive organs.

How is a baby started?

Before a new human can start to grow, a sperm and an ovum must join up. We call this <u>fertilisation</u>.

For an ovum to be fertilised, a man must put sperm inside a woman's body. This happens when they have sex.

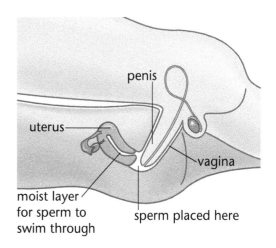

5 Look at the diagram. Then copy and complete the sentences.

A man puts sperm inside a woman's body through his _____. The sperm are put into the woman's _____, at the opening into her _____.

Ova are fertilised in the egg tube. The fertilised ovum grows inside the mother's uterus. After about 9 months the baby is ready to be born.

6 (a) What is fertilisation?

(b) Where does it usually happen?

7 How do sperm get to the egg tube from the opening of the uterus?

8 How long does it take for the fertilised ovum to grow into a baby which is ready to be born?

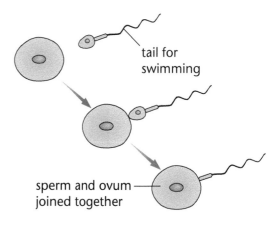

Fertilisation.

WHAT YOU NEED TO REMEMBER (Copy and complete using the **key words**)

Making babies

	Male	Female
Name of sex cells	_____	_____
Where the sex cells are made	_____	_____
Opening to the outside	a tube through the _____	_____
Other organs	_____ to put the sperm in the woman's vagina	_____ where the baby grows

You need to be able to label diagrams of male and female reproductive organs.

More about pregnancy: C1.5

4.2 Growing and changing

Graham has been growing in his mother's womb (uterus) for nearly nine months. In a few weeks' time he will be born.

How did Graham start?

Graham started life as a **fertilised** ovum.

A fertilised ovum starts to develop straight away. The cell splits into two cells. These two cells then split again to make four. This carries on until there is a ball of cells.

After a few weeks you can see how the cells are making different parts of the new person.

1 What features of the new person can be seen at four weeks?

2 What features develop between two weeks and seven weeks?

REMEMBER from page 71

Every human being starts life as two sex cells. When an ovum and a sperm join together, they make a single fertilised ovum.

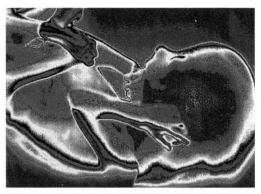

A scan of a baby inside his mother's uterus.

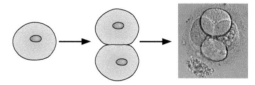

Cells split over and over again.

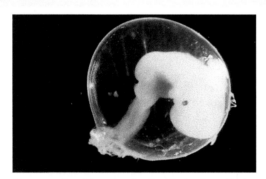

Four weeks. The developing baby is called an embryo.

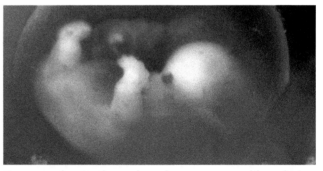

Seven weeks. As the embryo becomes more like a baby, we call it a fetus.

The new baby

Graham is now three months old. He needs his parents to do everything for him. They still have to feed him in the night sometimes.

Three months after birth.

Growing up

More changes will happen as Graham gets older.

When a girl is an adolescent her ovaries start to release eggs.

*As a baby Graham grows. He learns to control his body. As a young **child** he walks and uses his hands. He has learnt to talk.*

*When he is an **adolescent** Graham's testes start to make sperm.*

When he is a fully grown adult, Graham may marry and produce children of his own. So we start at the beginning of the cycle again.

3 What will happen to Graham when he is an adolescent?

4 Draw a chart to show the main changes in your life so far.
Then add what might happen as you get older.

Old age

Graham's grandfather spends time playing with Graham. He helps to look after him.

Graham's grandfather has a lot of knowledge and experience of life. He can pass this on to Graham to help him as he grows up.

5 Write down <u>three</u> ways a grandparent can help a child.

WHAT YOU NEED TO REMEMBER (Copy and complete using the **key words**)

Growing and changing

Copy and complete the diagram to show all the stages in a human life cycle.

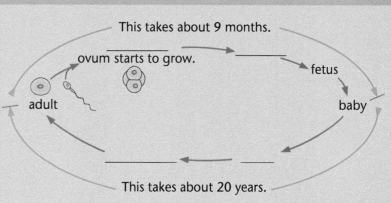

This takes about 9 months.

ovum starts to grow.

fetus

adult

baby

This takes about 20 years.

More about life cycles: C1.4

4.3 Growing pains

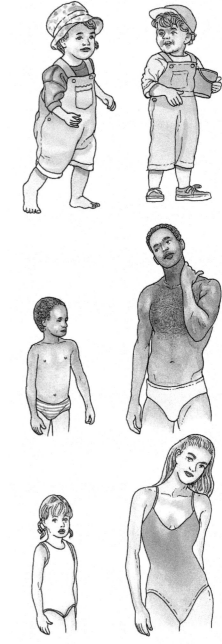

When they are very small, girls and boys look quite similar. Their bodies are the same shape.

But as children grow up, their bodies **change**. They start to look more like adult women and men. The time when these changes happen is called **puberty**.

1 Copy and complete the sentence.

Puberty is the time when girls start to change into _____ and _____ start to change into men.

■ How do people's bodies change?

The pictures show some of the differences between the bodies of adults and children.

2 Write down <u>three</u> differences you can see between:

(a) the man's body and the boy's body;

(b) the woman's body and the girl's body.

The table shows some of the other changes that happen at puberty.

3 **(a)** Write down <u>two</u> changes that are exactly the same for boys and girls.

(b) Write down <u>one</u> change that is different for girls and boys but is the same <u>sort</u> of change.

(c) Write down <u>one</u> change which applies only to boys.

Other changes during puberty	
Girls	**Boys**
hair grows under arms	hair grows under arms
pubic hair grows (around vagina)	pubic hair grows (around penis)
ovaries start to release ova	testes start to make sperm
monthly periods (of bleeding) begin	penis grows bigger
	voice deepens

A woman's monthly cycle

When a girl changes into a woman, an egg is released each month from one of her ovaries. Her monthly periods also begin.

4 Look at the diagram.

(a) What is happening during a woman's monthly bleeding period?

(b) What happens in the uterus in the week after the period of bleeding?

(c) What happens about halfway through each monthly cycle?

This monthly cycle of events is called the **menstrual cycle**.

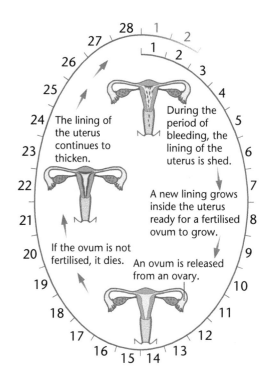

The menstrual cycle.

Text within diagram:

During the period of bleeding, the lining of the uterus is shed.

The lining of the uterus continues to thicken.

A new lining grows inside the uterus ready for a fertilised ovum to grow.

If the ovum is not fertilised, it dies.

An ovum is released from an ovary.

When does puberty occur?

Puberty doesn't happen at the same time for everyone.

Girls can start to change from about the age of 9. Most girls notice a lot of changes in their bodies from age 11 to 14. Most boys start to change at about 11 years old. Later, at about 16, they start to grow hair on their face and become more muscular.

5 Many teenagers find puberty a difficult time. Write down <u>one</u> reason for this.

6 At 10 Gemma's breasts have started to develop. At 14 Shane's pubic hair has not started to grow.

(a) Why might Gemma and Shane be worried?

(b) Why is there no real need to worry?

Some teenagers get spots. This can upset them when they have started to care about how they look. The problem clears up by itself after a few years.

WHAT YOU NEED TO REMEMBER (Copy and complete using the **key words**)

Growing pains

Our bodies _____ as we grow. Sometimes it is hard to adapt to these changes.

Boys and girls start to make sex cells at the time of _____. Girls start their _____ _____ and they have a period (of bleeding) about once a month.

More about the human life cycle: C1.4

4.4 A new plant life

Flowering plants grow from seeds.

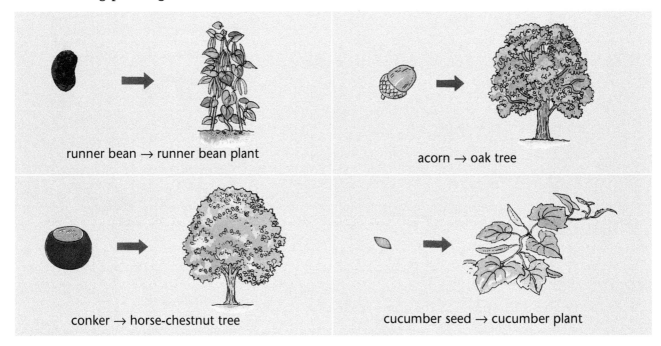

runner bean → runner bean plant

acorn → oak tree

conker → horse-chestnut tree

cucumber seed → cucumber plant

1 What flowering plant grows from:

(a) an acorn;

(b) a conker?

What is in a seed?

Seeds from different plants are different sizes, shapes and colours. But they all have the same basic parts.

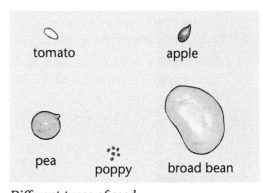

tomato

apple

pea

poppy

broad bean

Different types of seed.

Look at the diagram. It shows a bean seed cut open, right down the middle.

2 A seed contains a very tiny plant. What is this tiny plant called?

3 Why does the seed need a food store?

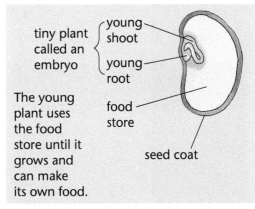

tiny plant called an embryo

young shoot

young root

The young plant uses the food store until it grows and can make its own food.

food store

seed coat

Bean seed cut in half.

Starting to grow

If a seed is given the things it needs, it will start to grow. We say that it <u>germinates</u>.

The diagram shows what happens to the seed. This is the plant's life cycle.

The life cycle of a flowering plant.

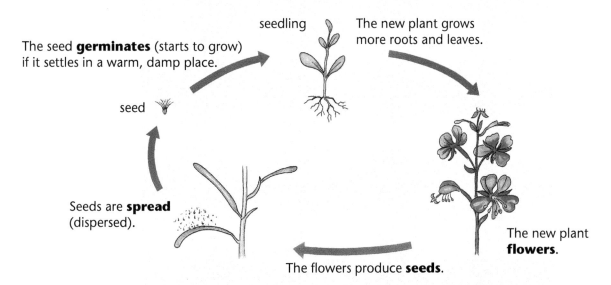

seedling

The new plant grows more roots and leaves.

The seed **germinates** (starts to grow) if it settles in a warm, damp place.

seed

The new plant **flowers**.

Seeds are **spread** (dispersed).

The flowers produce **seeds**.

4 What <u>two</u> things do seeds need so they can start to grow?

5 Plants grow roots, stems and leaves. Then they flower. Which of these parts of a plant makes the seeds?

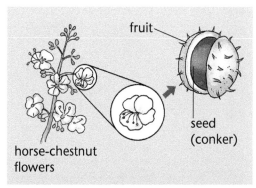

fruit

seed (conker)

horse-chestnut flowers

WHAT YOU NEED TO REMEMBER (Copy and complete using the **key words**)

A new plant life

The life cycle of a flowering plant.

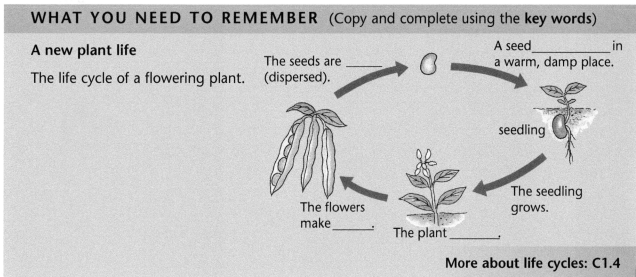

The seeds are _____ (dispersed).

A seed_____in a warm, damp place.

seedling

The seedling grows.

The flowers make_____.

The plant_____.

More about life cycles: C1.4

77

4.5 Looking at a plant's sex organs

Many plants grow from seeds. Seeds are made by flowers. So flowers are the parts of plants that are used for reproduction.

Flowers have male and female parts. These male and female parts are often on the <u>same</u> flower.

1 (a) What are the female parts of the flower?

(b) What are the male parts?

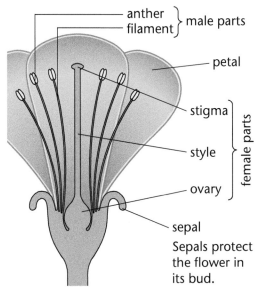

anther
filament } male parts

petal

stigma
style
ovary } female parts

sepal

Sepals protect the flower in its bud.

▪ Comparing different flowers

Flowers from different plants look different from each other. But they all have the same basic parts.

Violet

Hibiscus

Daylily

Peony

2 Write down <u>three</u> ways in which flowers can be different from each other.

The diagram shows a primrose flower.

3 On a copy of the primrose flower:

(a) label the female parts;

(b) label the male parts.

4 Write down <u>two</u> differences between the primrose flower and the flower at the top of the page.

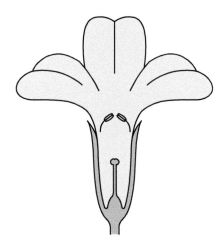
A primrose flower.

What do the male parts do?

Inside each pollen grain is a special cell. This is the plant's male sex cell.

5 **(a)** What are the flower's male sex cells inside?

   (b) Where in the flower are these made?

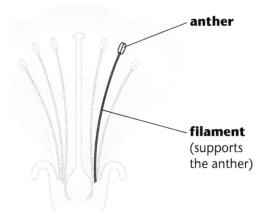

The male parts of a flower.

anther

filament (supports the anther)

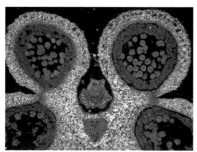

This anther has four pollen sacs.

Pollen sacs have many pollen grains. This shows them magnified 250 times.

The female parts of a flower

Each ovule has a female sex cell inside it.

6 Where in the flower are the ovules?

To make a seed, a male sex cell must join with a female sex cell.

7 Where on a flower does pollen land?

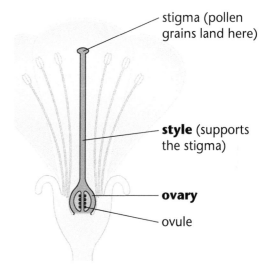

The female parts of a flower.

stigma (pollen grains land here)

style (supports the stigma)

ovary

ovule

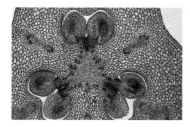

Many ovules can grow inside the ovary. This photograph shows them magnified 60 times.

WHAT YOU NEED TO REMEMBER (Copy and complete using the **key words**)

Looking at a plant's sex organs

You need to be able to label a diagram of a flower.

Flower part	What it does
_____	Pollen is made here.
_____	This supports the anther.
_____	This supports the stigma.
_____	Ovules are made here.

More about plant reproduction: C1.6

4.6 Making seeds

New flowering plants grow from **seeds**.

To make seeds, **pollen** must first travel from the anther to the stigma.

1 Copy and complete the sentences.

Pollen is made in the _____ of a flower.

It _____ to another flower of the same kind.

When pollen lands on the stigma of this other flower we call it _____.

Some plants have flowers which can pollinate themselves.

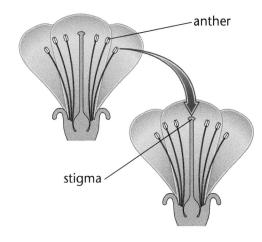

*Pollen travels from an anther to a stigma. This is called **pollination**.*

How does the pollen travel?

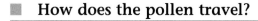

Some flowers use insects to move their pollen.

The insects get food and the flowers get their pollen carried to other flowers.

2 What <u>three</u> things can attract an insect to a flower?

3 Insects transfer pollen from one plant to another by accident. Explain, as fully as you can, how this happens.

Pollination by insects.

Insects are attracted by the bright colour of petals or by the flower's scent.

anther

Inside, the insect picks up pollen on its body. The pollen is sticky to help this.

This flower has nectar at the bottom. Some insects go into the flower to feed on the nectar.

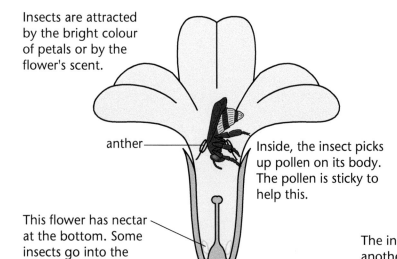

stigma

The insect goes to another flower. Pollen on its body is transferred to the stigma of this flower.

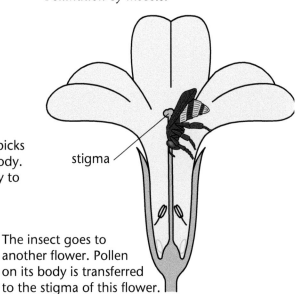

Moving pollen by the wind

The diagram shows a flower that does not attract insects. Instead, pollen is carried between these types of flowers by the wind.

4 Write down <u>two</u> ways this flower is adapted for pollination by wind.

5 Why doesn't this flower have brightly coloured petals or a strong scent?

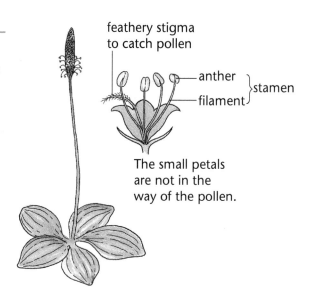

feathery stigma to catch pollen

anther
filament } stamen

The small petals are not in the way of the pollen.

What happens after pollination?

As soon as pollen lands on a stigma, a tube starts to grow from it.

The male sex cell now goes down to the **ovule** and joins with the female sex cell.

The two cells join together to make a single cell. We call this **fertilisation**. It is the beginning of a new seed. Remember, this is how a new animal starts life too.

The diagrams show how all this happens.

6 A plant has just been pollinated. How does fertilisation then happen?

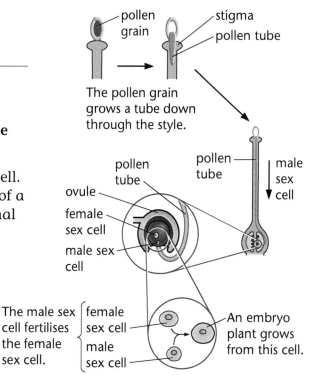

pollen grain — stigma — pollen tube

The pollen grain grows a tube down through the style.

pollen tube — pollen tube — male sex cell

ovule
female sex cell
male sex cell

The male sex cell fertilises the female sex cell. { female sex cell / male sex cell }

An embryo plant grows from this cell.

WHAT YOU NEED TO REMEMBER (Copy and complete using the **key words**)

Making seeds

Flowering plants grow from _____. Seeds are made inside the flower.

First, _____ is moved from an anther to a stigma. We call this _____.

The male sex cell nucleus inside the pollen joins with the female sex cell nucleus inside an _____. We call this _____.

More about making seeds: C1.6

4.7 What is a species?

There are many different kinds of plants and animals. We call each different kind a **species**.

Each species of plant or animal must be able to reproduce or it will die out.

Sorting animals into species

The pictures show six animals.

Kris and Sam decide to sort them into groups. This is how they do it.

Kris's table

Black	White	Ginger

Sam's table

Dogs	Cats

1 Copy and complete the tables for Kris and Sam.

2 (a) Who sorted the animals into their species?

   (b) Why is this a more useful way of sorting the animals?

Animals of the same species are similar and do the same sorts of things. They can also mate with each other and produce young.

Pekinese.

Burmese white.

Terrier.

Labrador.

Ginger tabby.

Persian.

Having young

A female cat can mate with a male cat and produce kittens. This is because the female cat and the male cat belong to the same species.

A cat cannot mate with a dog. This is because they belong to different species. We say that cats and dogs cannot **interbreed**.

male wild rabbit

female hare

female Dutch rabbit

3 Look at the pictures.

(a) Which animal will interbreed with the male wild rabbit?

(b) Write down <u>one</u> reason for your answer.

Are horses and donkeys different species?

Sometimes animals from slightly different species do try to mate. In some cases they are successful.

Horses and donkeys sometimes mate. The young are not horses or donkeys. They are something in between.

horse

donkey

4 Look at the pictures. What do we call the young produced when a horse and a donkey mate?

When young mules grow up they cannot breed. We say that mules are <u>infertile</u>. So we still call horses and donkeys different species because they cannot breed to produce **fertile** offspring.

5 If people want more mules, how do they get them?

mule

WHAT YOU NEED TO REMEMBER (Copy and complete using the **key words**)

What is a species?

A species is one kind of living thing. It differs from other _____ and it cannot _____ with them to produce _____ offspring.

More about species: C1.9

4.8 We are all different

Humans are different from each other in lots of ways. They **vary** a lot. But they can interbreed so all humans belong to the same **species**.

1 Write down <u>three</u> ways in which some of these girls are different from the others.

The things you have described in your answers are called features or **characteristics**.

The identity parade

The owners of a flat saw a girl breaking in. They described her to the police.

2 Look at her picture, then write your own description of her.

The police thought that they knew who the burglar was. Her name is Gail.

The owners of the flat picked out Gail in an identity parade. But the police needed other evidence that she was the right girl.

3 Look at the picture. Write down <u>two</u> pieces of evidence that the police found.

The suspect, Gail.

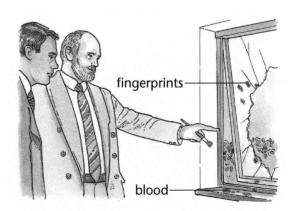

fingerprints

blood

The blood

Everyone fits into one of four blood groups: A, B, AB and O.

4 Look at the chart. Write down the percentage of people in each blood group.

5 (a) Gail's blood is group O. If the blood on the window is also group O, it does not prove that Gail was the burglar. Why is this?

(b) What does it tell the police?

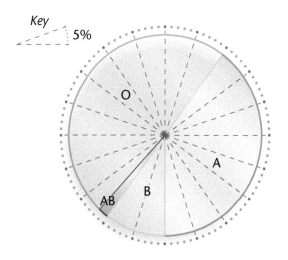

Key
5%

Percentage of people in the UK with each blood group.

The fingerprints

We all have different fingerprints. So, if the police find Gail's fingerprints at the scene of the crime, they will know that she was there.

6 Look at the fingerprints.

(a) Which fingerprint is like Gail's?

(b) Write a sentence about what this tells the police.

7 Write a list of evidence against Gail that the police can use in court.

Fingerprints found on the window.

Gail's fingerprint.

> Find out:
> ■ the difference between continuous and discontinuous variation.
> ■ of which of these two kinds of variation is blood group an example?

WHAT YOU NEED TO REMEMBER (Copy and complete using the **key words**)

We are all different

Members of a species can be different in many ways.
We say they _____ or they have different _____.
But they are still members of the same species if they can _____.

All humans belong to the same _____.

More about variation: C1.9

5.1 Night-time and day-time animals

You can see some animals, like squirrels, in the daytime. At night you see other animals, such as bats and owls.

The charts show some differences between the day and the night. We call these different <u>conditions</u>.

1 What do we call the time of day when it is:

(a) getting light;

(b) getting dark?

2 At what time of day is it warmest and lightest?

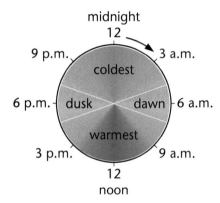

■ Animals of the night

Foxes often sleep during the day. They hunt for food at night. Foxes love eating earthworms. Earthworms only come up out of the soil when it is **cool** and **dark**.

3 Foxes find lots of earthworms at night. Why is this?

4 Write down <u>two</u> reasons why earthworms are likely to die if they come up during the day.

We call animals that are active at night <u>nocturnal</u> animals.

5 Write down the names of <u>three</u> nocturnal animals.

Earthworms mate above ground at night. They may dry up and die if they come up during the day.

Foxes use their senses of smell, hearing and sight when hunting.

Animals of the day

House sparrows are common in towns. They start feeding as soon as it begins to get light. They shelter at night when it is cold and dark.

Kestrels need good light to hunt for food. One of their favourite foods is sparrows.

6 At what times are sparrows most in danger of being eaten by kestrels?

Kestrels feed when it is light.

Senses for finding food

Animals use their senses for finding food. Some senses are more useful during the day and others at night. Animals' senses are **adapted** to the time of day that they hunt.

7 Copy and complete the table.

Animal	Senses it uses to find food
fox	
bat	
owl	
kestrel	

You can see foxes, owls and kestrels all the year round.

Bats eat insects, so you don't see them in the winter when there are hardly any insects for them to feed on.

Bats hunt by sending out sound and listening for echoes.

Owls hear well and can see in dim light.

WHAT YOU NEED TO REMEMBER (Copy and complete using the **key words**)

Night-time and day-time animals

Some animals are _____ for feeding during the day.
Other animals feed at night when it is _____ and _____.

More about daily change: C3.1

5.2 How animals and plants survive the winter

In winter the days are short, and it is often very **cold**. Animals and plants do different things to survive the winter. We say they are **adapted** in different ways.

1 The pictures show the same place in winter and summer. Write down <u>three</u> differences you can see.

Animals in winter

In winter some British animals, such as bats, go into a deep sleep: they <u>hibernate</u>.

Other animals go to a warmer country: they <u>migrate</u>.

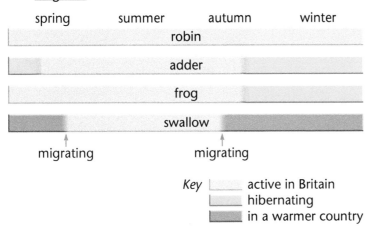

We call the different parts of each year **seasons**. We see different animals in different seasons. Look at the diagram.

Even in summer adders need to sunbathe until they are warm enough to go hunting.

2 Which animal can we see in the UK all the year round?

3 **(a)** During which seasons are adders active?

(b) Why can't they hunt in the winter?

4 Write down the names of <u>two</u> animals which hibernate.

5 Write down <u>two</u> reasons why swallows migrate to Africa.

When it is winter in Britain, it is summer in Africa. So it is warm and swallows can find lots of insects to eat.

Plants in winter

Plants also do different things in different seasons. Look at the pictures of an apple tree.

6 For each season, write down one sentence about the tree.

Different plants have different ways of surviving the winter.

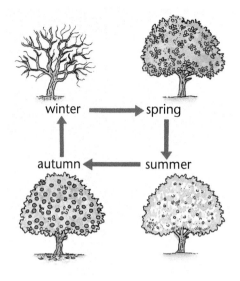

winter ➡ spring

autumn ⬅ summer

spring   summer   autumn   winter

apple tree

poppy

New plants grow from seeds.   Only the seeds survive.

bluebell

The bulb is alive under the ground.

pine tree

Key ▭ has green leaves and makes food
▭ doesn't make food or grow

7 Describe what each of the plants in the diagram does to survive the winter.

Bluebells are adapted to living in woods.

8 When do bluebells finish growing?

9 Why can't bluebells get enough light in the summer?

Plants under trees cannot make enough food when tree leaves block the light.

WHAT YOU NEED TO REMEMBER (Copy and complete using the **key words**)

How animals and plants survive the winter

The different parts of the year are called _____.

In winter there is less light and it can be very _____.

Plants and animals are _____ in different ways to survive the winter.

More about seasonal change: C3.1

5.3 Town and country

Town.

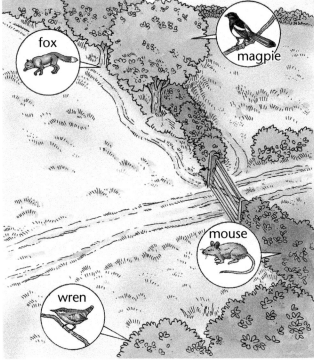

Countryside.

Many people think that wild plants and animals live only in the countryside. But lots of wild plants and animals also live in towns.

Look at the pictures above.

1 For each picture, write down <u>three</u> different places where plants and animals can live.

The place where a plant or animal lives is called its **habitat**. A habitat provides space and shelter.

2 Is the number of different habitats greater in the town picture or the country picture?

3 Copy and complete the sentences.

Where there are lots of different _____,
lots of different plants and _____ can live.
So more species live in a square kilometre of a town than in the same area of _____.

Key
▢ farm and pet animals
▨ food waste from kitchens
▨ wild birds and mammals
▨ insects
▢ earthworms
▨ fruit and vegetables

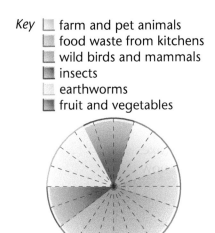

What a country fox eats.

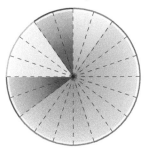

What a town fox eats.

■ Town fox, country fox

When young foxes grow up, they have to find a habitat which has everything they need. Lots of young foxes moved from the countryside into towns. So foxes are now more common in towns than in the countryside.

The pictures show two ways that a fox can get the **shelter** it needs.

4 Write down <u>two</u> ways in which these shelters are similar.

5 Why must the habitat of a fox contain somewhere to shelter or hide?

A town fox.

A fox's habitat must also supply the **food** it needs to live and grow.

6 Look at the pie charts on page 90.

  (a) Write down the <u>two</u> main types of food which a country fox eats.

  (b) Write down the <u>two</u> main types of food which a town fox eats.

7 Copy and complete the sentences.

Most foxes used to live in the _____. Many foxes now live in _____.

They have learned to find the _____ and _____ that they need.

A fox in the country lives in an <u>earth</u>.

WHAT YOU NEED TO REMEMBER (Copy and complete using the **key words**)

Town and country

The place where a plant or animal lives is called its _____.
A habitat must provide _____ and a source of _____.

More about habitats: C3.6

91

5.4 Different bodies for different habitats

Different animals and plants live in different **habitats**. Their bodies are **adapted** so they can survive in their habitats.

Bodies designed for moving

The bodies of animals and plants have **features** suited to where they live and what they do.

Plants don't move from place to place, but animals do.

1 Look at the pictures. Write down <u>three</u> reasons why animals need to move.

2 An earthworm is adapted for burrowing in soil. Explain why its shape is good for burrowing.

A mole is adapted for burrowing in a different way. It has a skeleton, and muscles to pull on the bones. Look at the pictures.

3 Write down <u>two</u> ways the mole's skeleton is adapted for its way of life.

REMEMBER from page 90

The place where a plant or animal lives is called its habitat.

hunting   escaping

finding a mate

finding food

Why animals move.

pointed 'head' end

An earthworm has a long, thin body and a slimy skin.

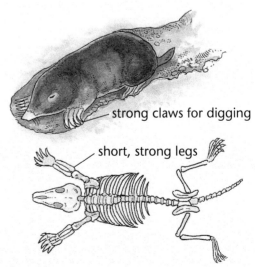

strong claws for digging

short, strong legs

A mole.

Bodies designed for support

A skeleton isn't just for movement. It also holds an animal together in the right shape. We say it <u>supports</u> the animal.

Elephant and whale skeletons drawn to the same scale.

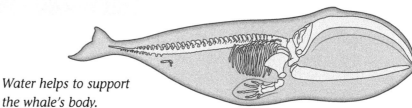

4 Look at the diagrams.

   (a) Which animal is bigger, an elephant or a whale?

   (b) Why does an elephant need a stronger skeleton than a whale?

Water helps to support the whale's body.

Plants need support too

Water helps to support water plants as well as animals.

5 Look at the pictures. Write down <u>two</u> differences between the land plant and the water plant.

Plants have roots to anchor them in soil or mud. Some plants also have woody stems to make them stronger.

6 Suggest <u>one</u> reason for <u>each</u> of the differences you described in your answer to question 5.

Water plant.   Land plant.

WHAT YOU NEED TO REMEMBER (Copy and complete using the **key words**)

Different bodies for different habitats

Different plants and animals live in different _____.

Plants and animals have _____ which suit them to the places they live.
We say that they are _____ to their habitats.

More about adaptation: C3.6

5.5 Surviving in a garden

The compost heap in the drawing is just one of the <u>habitats</u> in the garden. Lots of earthworms, woodlice and millipedes live there.

1 Write down <u>three</u> other habitats you can see in the drawing.

Worms, spiders and beetles live in all parts of the garden, but the ones in the pond are different from the ones which live in the flower bed. Their bodies have **features** which suit them to the places they live. We say that each kind is **adapted** to its own habitat.

2 Look at the pictures. Write down <u>two</u> ways the compost worm is different from the earthworm.

Ways of getting oxygen

All animals need oxygen.

Some use oxygen from the air. Others use oxygen dissolved in the water.

Earthworms take in oxygen from the air through their damp skins.

Like all beetles, water beetles get their oxygen from the air. Their bodies are adapted to do this under the water.

3 How can water beetles get air under water?

4 Why do water beetles keep coming up to the surface of a pond?

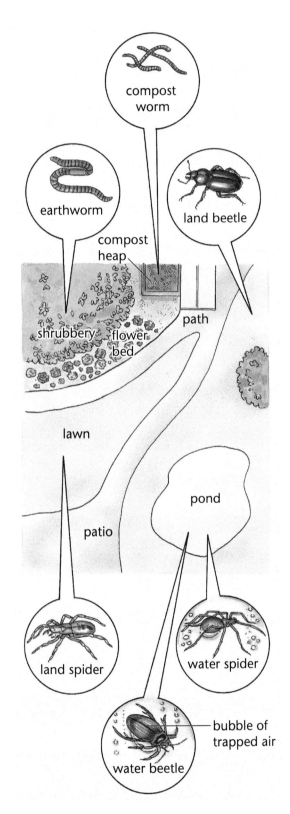

compost worm

earthworm

land beetle

compost heap

shrubbery flower bed path

lawn

pond

patio

land spider

water spider

water beetle — bubble of trapped air

Ways of getting food

Beetles and spiders feed on other animals so we call them <u>predators</u>.

Beetles have jaws to cut up their food. Spiders suck the juices from their prey. Their jaws are adapted to these different ways of feeding.

5 Look at the pictures. Which jaws, A or B, belong to the spider? Explain your answer.

Plants make their own food. They take in carbon dioxide, water and minerals to do this.

6 How do plants take in the carbon dioxide, water and minerals they need?

A: these jaws cut up prey.

B: these jaws make a hole in the prey.

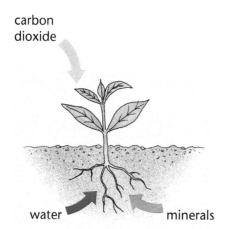

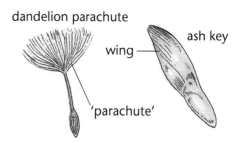

Adapted to be spread by the wind.

How do plants get to different places?

Because they have roots, plants can't move. So, many plants make <u>seeds</u> which can be moved.

7 Write down <u>two</u> ways plant seeds are adapted to reach new places.

Adapted to be spread by animals.

WHAT YOU NEED TO REMEMBER (Copy and complete using the **key words**)

Surviving in a garden

Plants and animals have _____ which suit them to the places they live and for what they do. We say they are _____ to their habitats and their way of life.

More about adaptation: C3.6

5.6 Feeding on plants

Only green plants can make food. So all <u>animals</u> depend on green plants to stay alive.

Even a flea which feeds only on mouse blood depends on green plants for its food. The diagram shows why this is.

1 Copy and complete the sentences.

The green plants are eaten by the _____ and the mouse's blood is _____ by the flea. This means that both the _____ and the _____ depend on the green _____ for food.

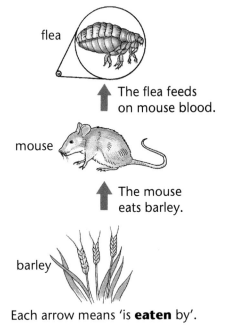

flea — The flea feeds on mouse blood.

mouse — The mouse eats barley.

barley

Each arrow means 'is **eaten** by'.

▇ Food chains

A diagram which shows who eats what is called a <u>food chain</u>. You can draw a food chain using words or pictures.

You always start with **green plants**, then show what **animals** eat. The arrows point the same way as the food goes.

2 What does the following food chain tell you?

ladybird
↑
greenfly
↑
leaf

3 Look at the photos. Then write a food chain to show who eats what.

hedgehog
snail

snail   lettuce

Food chains everywhere

There are food chains in every habitat. The diagrams show who eats what in different habitats.

4 Draw a food chain for each habitat. Make sure your arrows go in the same direction as the food.

The periwinkle has eaten the green seaweed from here.

periwinkle

crab

Seashore.

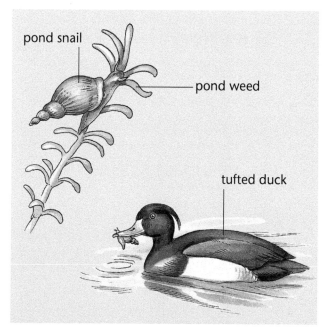

pond snail

pond weed

tufted duck

Pond.

owl

bank vole

blackberry

bramble bush

Woodland.

5 (a) What kind of living thing is at the <u>start</u> of each food chain?

(b) Why do all food chains start in this way?

WHAT YOU NEED TO REMEMBER (Copy and complete using the **key words**)

Feeding on plants

Food chains start with _____ _____. The rest of each food chain shows what _____ eat.

In a food chain, A → B → C means that A is _____ by B and B is eaten by C. We use the arrows to show the direction in which the food goes.

More about food chains: C3.5

5.7 Growing plants for food

Farmers and gardeners work hard to grow food crops. But a lot of food is lost to **pests**, diseases and weeds.

1 Look at the pie chart.

   (a) What percentage of a crop do people harvest in Africa?

   (b) What happens to the rest of a crop?

2 Use the information in the table to draw a similar pie chart for Europe. Start by splitting a circle in 5% segments (each 18° on a protractor).

Pesticides, fungicides and herbicides can harm other living things, including humans.

3 **(a)** How does the percentage lost in Europe compare with that in Africa?

   (b) Write down two possible reasons for the difference.

4 Write down one good thing and one bad thing about using pesticides.

Who's been eating the plants?

Sometimes a gardener find pests eating plants. Look at the pictures.

5 Write down the part of the plant which is eaten by:

   (a) the caterpillar,

   (b) the greenfly.

 Find a connection between Paul Müller, Rachel Carson and mosquitoes.

Key
▨ lost to pests   ▨ lost to weeds
▨ lost to diseases   ▨ harvested

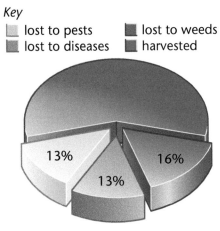

13%   16%
13%

Percentages of crops lost in Africa.

Percentages of crops lost in Europe.

Pests	Diseases	Weeds
5%	13%	7%

Pesticides	Fungicides	Herbicides
kill animals which eat crops	kill fungi	kill weeds

Greenflies suck sap from leaves.

Sometimes the gardener doesn't see what ate the plants. Many pests hide in the soil.

But she does know that different pests feed in different ways. Look at the photographs of the pests and the leaves they were eating.

6 Copy the drawing of the leaf and complete the labels.

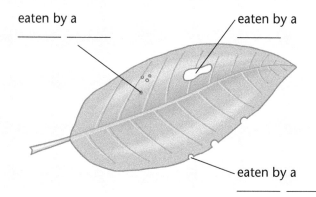

eaten by a
_____ _____

eaten by a
_____

eaten by a
_____ _____

Slugs make large holes in leaves.

Bean weevils eat the edges of leaves.

Flea beetles make small round holes.

■ Other animals eat the pests

Luckily for the gardener, even if she doesn't kill the pests, other animals eat them. We call these other animals **predators**.

7 Copy and complete the sentences.

Snails can do a lot of damage to garden plants. So gardeners like having _____ in their gardens.

Instead of spraying aphids with pesticides, a gardener could bring lots of _____ into the garden.

 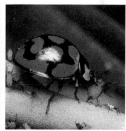

A hedgehog eating a snail.   *A ladybird eating an aphid.*

WHAT YOU NEED TO REMEMBER (Copy and complete using the **key words**)

Growing plants for food

Animals which eat the plants we grow for food are called _____.
We can kill them with chemicals called _____.

We can also encourage other animals to eat them. These animals are called _____.

More about food chains: C3.5

5.8 Predators, harmful and useful

REMEMBER from page 96

Food chains show what animals eat.

Some animals eat plants. Others eat animals. Animals which kill and eat other animals are called **predators**. The animals which get eaten are called **prey**.

1 Copy the table. Write in the names of two predators which live in gardens. Add the names of their prey.

Predator	Prey

Earthworms make soil more fertile, so plants grow better. Flatworms don't do this.

Plants don't grow well if greenfly are feeding on them.

2 Why don't gardeners want New Zealand flatworms in their gardens?

3 Why are they pleased to have ladybirds?

■ **Red spider mites**

Red spider mites are pests in greenhouses.

4 Write down one reason why gardeners don't want them.

5 Look at the food chain and write down the name of

(a) the predator;

(b) the prey.

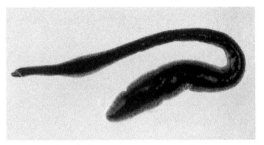

New Zealand flatworms eat earthworms.

New Zealand
flatworm   ladybird
↑   ↑

earthworm   greenfly
↑   ↑

dead leaves   plant sap

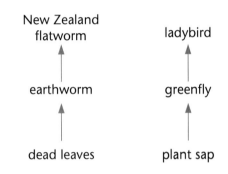

One kind of red spider mite. They do not all look as red as this one.

'Phyto'
↑

red spider mite
↑

cucumber plant

■ Making use of predators

Some students found red spider mites in a greenhouse where they were growing cucumbers.

They didn't want to use chemical pesticides to kill them because pesticides also kill useful animals such as ladybirds.

So they decided to put some predators of the mites into the greenhouse.

6 What would the predators do?

The graph shows how the number of red spider mites and predators **increases** and then **decreases.**

7 How many red spider mites were there when the students put the predators into the greenhouse?

8 On which day was the number of spider mites greatest?

9 The number of spider mites then fell quickly. What happened to them?

10 Copy and complete the sentences.

As the number of _____ _____ mites (prey) goes up, the number of predators also goes _____.
So, the number of red spider mites starts to decrease. Then the number of predators also _____.

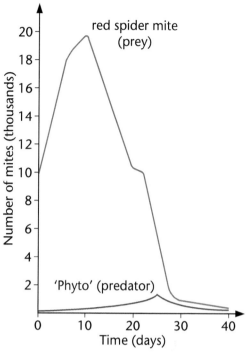

'Phyto' may be the predator but it is smaller than the red spider mite. The mite is less than a millimetre wide.

WHAT YOU NEED TO REMEMBER (Copy and complete using the **key words**)

Predators, harmful and useful

Animals which kill and eat other animals are called _____.
The animals they eat are called their _____.

If the number of prey increases, the number of predators also _____.
As the number of predators increases, the number of prey _____.

More about predators: C3.7

5.9 Garden food webs

REMEMBER from page 96

Food chains begin with green plants.

They show what animals eat.

Different pests often eat the same plant. This means that the plant is at the start of more than one **food chain**.

Food chains on a bramble plant.

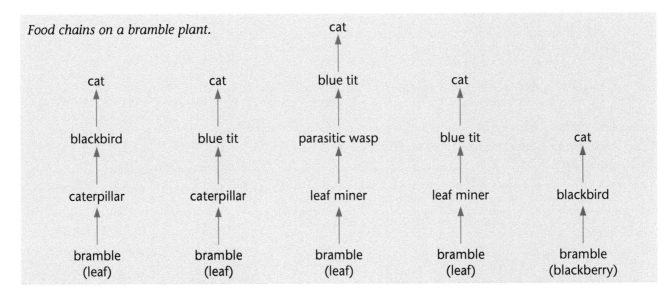

1 Write down the names of <u>two</u> pests that eat the leaves of a bramble plant.

In fact, most of the plants and animals in a garden belong to more than one food chain.

2 Look at the diagrams. What do all these food chains start with?

3 Write down the name of an animal which belongs to <u>two</u> food chains.

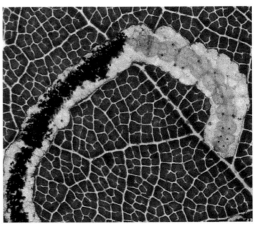

A leaf miner makes a burrow in a leaf. It eats the middle layers.

◼ Making a food web

We can join these food chains to make a **food web**. This shows more clearly what happens in a particular **habitat** or place.

4 Copy and complete the food web, starting with the bramble plant.

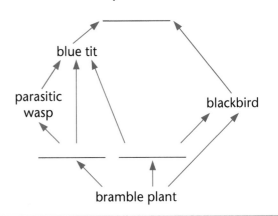

■ What's eating the pea plants?

A gardener wanted to grow peas so he planted a row of seeds. Mice and sparrows ate some of the seeds before they could even grow.

Look at the picture. It shows some of the other pests which feed on the pea plants.

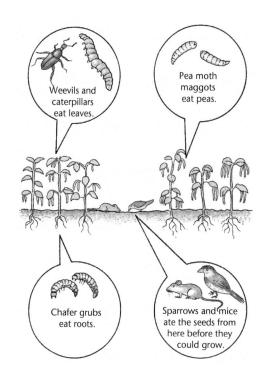

Weevils and caterpillars eat leaves.

Pea moth maggots eat peas.

Chafer grubs eat roots.

Sparrows and mice ate the seeds from here before they could grow.

5 Copy and complete the table.

Pest	Part of the pea plant that it eats
mouse	
sparrow	
pea moth maggot	
weevil	
caterpillar	
chafer grub	

6 Copy the food web.

(a) Write in the boxes the names of the pests that eat the pea plant.

(b) Look at the pictures of animals which eat these pests. Add their names to the food web.

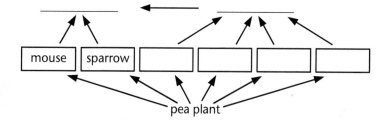

mouse | sparrow | | | |

pea plant

7 (a) Write down one of the longest food chains you can find in your food web.

(b) How many others are the same length?

Cat.

Blackbird.

WHAT YOU NEED TO REMEMBER (Copy and complete using the **key words**)

Garden food webs

In a habitat, plants and animals belong to more than one _____ _____.
This is why a _____ _____ is better for showing what eats what in a particular _____.

More about food webs: C3.5

103

5.10 Competition

All animals need a place to live. Often they have to **compete** with other animals for **space** and **food**.

Many animals, or groups of animals, have an area of their own. They chase away other animals of their own kind.

1 Look at the pictures. Write down <u>two</u> reasons why animals need space.

The space which an animal defends is called its <u>territory</u>.

2 Penguins feed on fish from the sea. Why do you think they need only a small territory on land?

A pair of robins defends a territory about half the size of a football pitch.

3 Why do such small birds need so much space?

■ How do animals mark their territories?

People often put fences around their homes to show how much space is theirs. Animals need to show other animals too. Different animals do this in different ways.

4 Look at the pictures, then copy and complete the sentences.

Robins _____ at the edges of their territories. Otters and _____ mark their territories with _____ and _____ substances from their bodies.

Penguins defend a small space to keep their eggs and young safe.

Robins sing to keep other robins out of their feeding space.

Groups of rabbits scent-mark their territories with a smelly substance from under their chins. They also use their urine and droppings.

Otters also scent-mark their territory.

Competition between plants

Plants also compete with each other for **space** and the other things they need.

5 Look at the diagram, then copy and complete the sentences.

Plants compete for the _____ and _____ in the soil. Above the ground, they _____ for _____ and carbon dioxide.

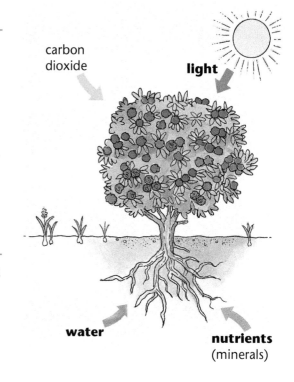

carbon dioxide

light

water

nutrients (minerals)

The problem of rhododendrons

Explorers brought rhododendrons to Britain from Asia many years ago.

They grow so well in Britain that they have spread from people's gardens into woodland. Other plants, such as bluebells, cannot compete with them.

6 Look at the picture.

(a) Write down <u>three</u> things which bluebells and rhododendrons compete for.

(b) What happens to bluebells in woods as rhododendrons spread?

Rhododendrons affect animals too. Few insects eat the tough leaves.

If there are fewer insects in a wood, there are also fewer birds.

7 Ecologists think that we should get rid of all the rhododendrons from our woods. Why is this?

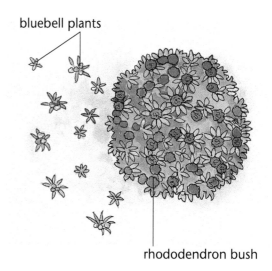

bluebell plants

rhododendron bush

WHAT YOU NEED TO REMEMBER (Copy and complete using the **key words**)

Competition

Animals _____ with each other for _____ and _____.

Plants compete with each other for _____, _____, _____ and _____.

More about competition: C3.7

C1.1 Cells

Every living thing is made up of small units called **cells**.

Look at the photograph of plant root cells.
It has been magnified many times so that you can see the cells.

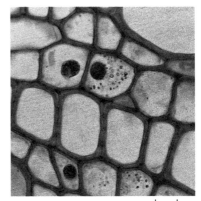

Plant root cells. 0.01 mm

1 Copy and complete the sentences.

The plant root is made of small _____.
Each cell is about _____ of a millimetre across.

Animal and plant cells

Animals and plants are made from cells.

Animal and plant cells are the same in some ways.
We say that they have some of the same <u>features</u>.

Animal and plant cells are also different in some ways.

 Robert Hooke was the first person to see and name cells. Why did he call them 'cells'?

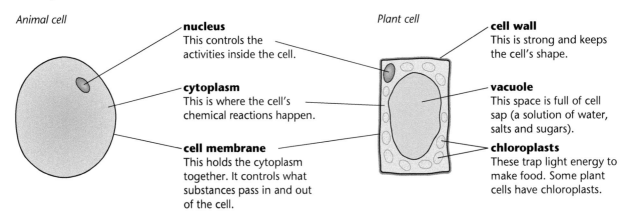

Animal cell

nucleus
This controls the activities inside the cell.

cytoplasm
This is where the cell's chemical reactions happen.

cell membrane
This holds the cytoplasm together. It controls what substances pass in and out of the cell.

Plant cell

cell wall
This is strong and keeps the cell's shape.

vacuole
This space is full of cell sap (a solution of water, salts and sugars).

chloroplasts
These trap light energy to make food. Some plant cells have chloroplasts.

2 What job do these parts of a cell do?

(a) the nucleus

(b) the cytoplasm

(c) the cell membrane

3 Copy the table. Then complete it to show differences between animal and plant cells.

Feature	Animal cell	Plant cell
Does it have a nucleus?	yes	
Does it have a cell membrane?		
Does it have cytoplasm?		
Does it have a cell wall?		
Does it have a vacuole?	no	
Does it have chloroplasts?		some plant cells do

Living things with only one cell

Some very simple living things are made of only one cell. We say they are **unicellular**.

Some unicellular organisms are like animals, but others are more like plants.

4 Look at the photographs.

   (a) Which cell, A, B or C, is most like a plant?

   (b) Write down <u>two</u> reasons for your answer.

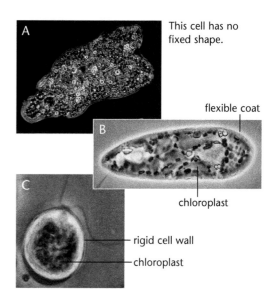

This cell has no fixed shape.

flexible coat

chloroplast

rigid cell wall

chloroplast

Living things with many cells

When a living organism is made up of many cells, we say it is **multicellular**.

Hydra is a simple multicellular animal. Its cells are not all the same. The *Hydra* needs different types of cell to do different jobs.

5 Write down <u>one</u> difference between unicellular and multicellular organisms.

6 Describe <u>two</u> different jobs done by two different types of cell in a *Hydra*.

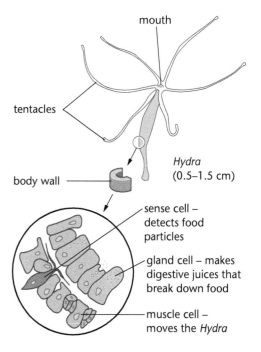

mouth

tentacles

body wall

Hydra (0.5–1.5 cm)

sense cell – detects food particles

gland cell – makes digestive juices that break down food

muscle cell – moves the *Hydra*

WHAT YOU NEED TO REMEMBER (Copy and complete using the **key words**)

Cells

Living things are made up of _____.

Some living things have only one cell; they are _____.
Living things with many cells are _____.

Both animal and plant cells have a _____, _____ and _____ _____.

Only plant cells have a _____ _____ and _____, and some plant cells have _____.

More about cells: CORE+ C1.10

Follows on from: 1.4

C1.2 Working together

Your body is made of millions of cells.

Each cell has its own special **job** to do, but it doesn't work on its own.

▪ Cells work together

Cells that do the same job are often grouped together. A group of similar cells is called a **tissue**. For example, muscle tissue is made up of lots of muscle cells.

1 Look at the description of a factory. Then copy and complete the sentences describing the human body.

A human body has millions of living _____ working in it. Each _____ has its own _____ to do. Cells of the same type join together to make a _____.

▪ Tissues work together

Different tissues join together to make **organs**, such as bones and muscles. For example, your biceps muscle is an organ. It pulls on bones to bend your arm.

2 Copy and complete the sentences.

My biceps is an _____, formed from several tissues joined together. Tissues in the biceps include _____, _____ and _____ tissue.

3 Copy and complete the table.

Tissue in the biceps (an organ)	What it does
	pulls lower part of arm upwards
epithelium tissue	
	connects muscle to bone

A large factory has many people working in it. The people work in <u>teams</u> to get things done. Each team has a particular <u>job</u> to do.

This is what the fibres in muscle tissue look like under a microscope.

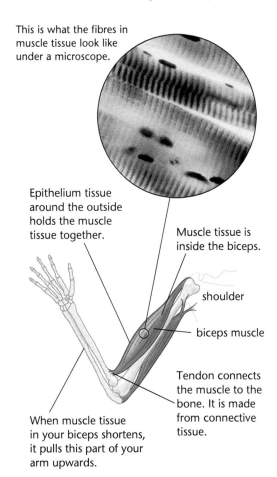

Epithelium tissue around the outside holds the muscle tissue together.

Muscle tissue is inside the biceps.

shoulder

biceps muscle

Tendon connects the muscle to the bone. It is made from connective tissue.

When muscle tissue in your biceps shortens, it pulls this part of your arm upwards.

Plants have tissues and organs too

<u>Xylem</u> is a type of tissue found in plants. Xylem cells join to form long tubes inside the plant. Each cell is tiny, but the tubes they make are very long. These tubes carry water to all parts of the plant.

4 Look at both the diagrams. Write down <u>three</u> reasons why xylem vessels are good at carrying water.

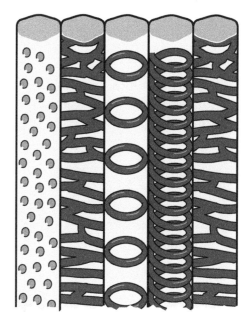

These xylem vessels go from the roots to the rest of the plant.

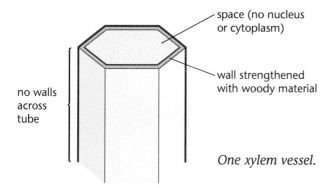

space (no nucleus or cytoplasm)

wall strengthened with woody material

no walls across tube

One xylem vessel.

The picture on the right shows where the xylem is in a root. A root is an organ, so it has other tissues too.

5 Copy and complete the table.

Tissue in a plant's root	What it does
xylem	
phloem	

 Find out the names of <u>two</u> other tissues in the plant root.
Add them to the table that you did for question 5.

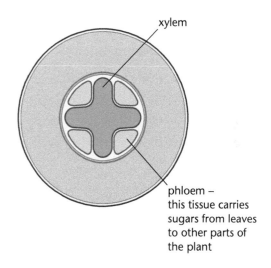

xylem

phloem – this tissue carries sugars from leaves to other parts of the plant

A slice through a root.

WHAT YOU NEED TO REMEMBER (Copy and complete using the **key words**)

Working together

We call groups of similar cells a _____.
Different tissues are grouped together into _____.

Cells, tissues and organs are all suited to the _____ they do.

More about tissues and organs: CORE+ C1.11

C1.3 Life processes

All living things, from the smallest to the biggest, must do certain things to stay alive. We call these things <u>life processes</u>.

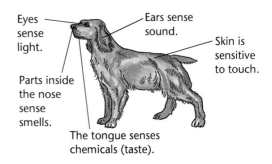

Eyes sense light.

Ears sense sound.

Skin is sensitive to touch.

Parts inside the nose sense smells.

The tongue senses chemicals (taste).

Sensitivity

Living things can **sense** changes around them.

1 Write down <u>five</u> things that a dog can sense.

2 Write down <u>two</u> things that plants are sensitive to.

> **DID YOU KNOW?**
>
> Your skin is sensitive to a change in temperature of only 0.5 °C.

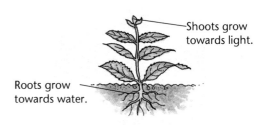

Shoots grow towards light.

Roots grow towards water.

Movement

Animals **move** to find food.

Plants don't need to do this. Some <u>parts</u> of plants move though.

Respiration

Living things need energy. They all get this energy from food and oxygen by respiration.

Animals and plants both **respire**.

3 Where in plants and animals does respiration happen?

4 What waste product is made when cells respire?

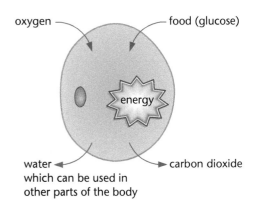

oxygen

food (glucose)

energy

water which can be used in other parts of the body

carbon dioxide

Respiration happens in cells.

Reproduction and growth

Living things eventually die. So they need to produce young. We say that they **reproduce**.

Young plants and animals then **grow** until they are old enough to reproduce themselves.

5 How many years do boys usually grow for?

height

3   8   13   18   adult

age (years)

Growing up.

Nutrition

All living things must have **nutrition** (food). It gives them the energy and materials they need to move and to make new cells. They make new cells all the time so they can grow, reproduce, and repair damage to the body.

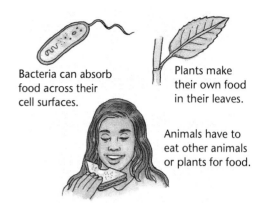

Bacteria can absorb food across their cell surfaces.

Plants make their own food in their leaves.

Animals have to eat other animals or plants for food.

6 Copy and complete the table.

Living things	How they get their food
bacteria	
plants	
animals	

Excretion

All living things make waste materials. These wastes are poisonous. You must get rid of them from your cells and your blood. Getting rid of waste is called <u>excretion</u>.

7 List <u>three</u> things you excrete from your body.

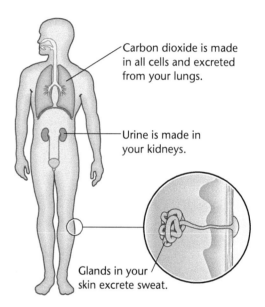

Carbon dioxide is made in all cells and excreted from your lungs.

Urine is made in your kidneys.

Glands in your skin excrete sweat.

*Humans **excrete** sweat, urine and carbon dioxide.*

What is special about living things?

Some non-living things move and can use oxygen to release energy from fuel. But non-living things cannot make new materials for their bodies. This means that they <u>cannot</u> **grow** or **reproduce**. Producing young that grow is something only living things can do.

MRS GREN can help you to remember:

M ovement   G rowth
R espiration   R eproduction
S ensitivity   E xcretion
               N utrition

DID YOU KNOW?

You <u>don't</u> excrete faeces. Undigested food never really gets inside your body. It just goes through a very long tube between your mouth and your anus.

WHAT YOU NEED TO REMEMBER (Copy and complete using the **key words**)

Life processes

Living things can s_____, m_____, r_____, g_____, r_____, e_____, and they need n_____.

Non-living things cannot _____ or _____.

C1.4 Cycles of life

All living things grow and change during their lives.

Flowering plants and many animals, including humans, start life as two special cells. These special cells are called <u>sex</u> <u>cells</u> or **gametes**.

For humans

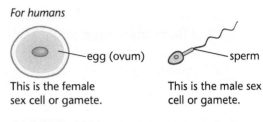

This is the female sex cell or gamete.

This is the male sex cell or gamete.

1 Copy and complete the table.

	Female sex cell	**Male sex cell**
humans	_____	_____
flowering plants	inside _____	inside _____

For flowering plants

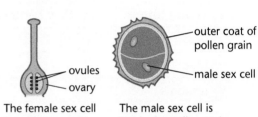

The female sex cell is inside an ovule.

The male sex cell is inside the pollen grain.

For a new human or plant to grow, the male and female sex cells must join together. The diagram shows what happens in a human.

The male and female sex cells join together.

A single cell with a single nucleus is formed.

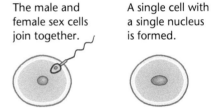

This process is called **fertilisation**.

2 Copy and complete the sentences.

A male gamete and a female gamete join together to make a single _____.
This process is called _____.

Getting plant sex cells together

Flowers produce sex cells. Male sex cells must meet up with female sex cells.
To make sure this happens, each part of a flower has a different job to do.

3 Copy and complete the table.

Flower part	**What it does**
anther	
filament	
stigma	
style	
ovary	
petal	
nectary	

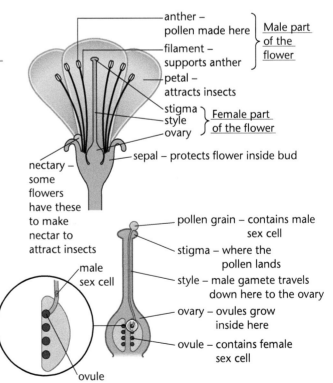

anther –
pollen made here } Male part of the flower

filament –
supports anther

petal –
attracts insects

stigma
style } Female part of the flower
ovary

sepal – protects flower inside bud

nectary – some flowers have these to make nectar to attract insects

pollen grain – contains male sex cell

stigma – where the pollen lands

style – male gamete travels down here to the ovary

ovary – ovules grow inside here

ovule – contains female sex cell

male sex cell

ovule

■ Sexual intercourse in humans

A new human develops inside a woman's body.

Sperm have to be placed inside her body so that one of them can reach the ovum and fertilise it. This happens during sexual intercourse.

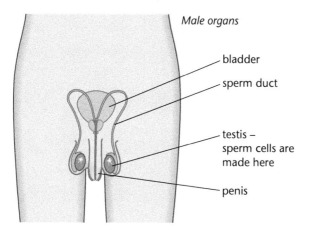

Male organs

- bladder
- sperm duct
- testis – sperm cells are made here
- penis

The sperm cells travel from the testes through to the penis. They are pushed into the vagina during sexual intercourse.

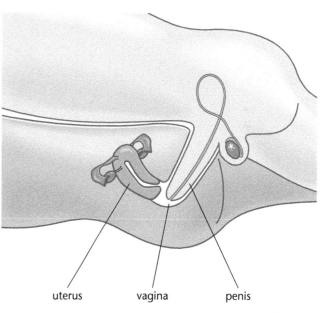

uterus   vagina   penis

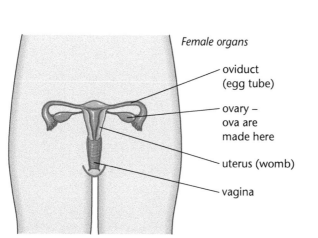

Female organs

- oviduct (egg tube)
- ovary – ova are made here
- uterus (womb)
- vagina

4 Where are human female sex cells made?

5 Where are human male sex cells made?

6 Copy and complete the sentences.

During sexual intercourse, sperm from a man's _____ travel through his _____.
They go into the woman's body through her _____.

WHAT YOU NEED TO REMEMBER (Copy and complete using the **key words**)

Cycles of life

The sexual reproductive systems of plants and animals make special sex cells or _____.

Gametes join together in a process we call _____.

Follows on from: 4.1

C1.5 The start of pregnancy

Ova are made in the ovaries. A woman releases an ovum from one of her ovaries once a month. The ovum travels down the **oviduct** (egg tube). If the ovum meets a sperm, they may join together. We call this **fertilisation**. From this moment the woman's pregnancy begins.

REMEMBER from page 113

Sexual intercourse is a way of bringing the sperm and ovum together. The man puts his penis inside the woman's vagina and pushes millions of **sperm** into her.

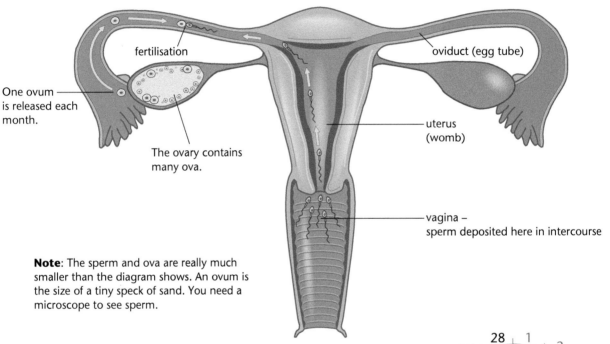

fertilisation

oviduct (egg tube)

One ovum is released each month.

The ovary contains many ova.

uterus (womb)

vagina – sperm deposited here in intercourse

Note: The sperm and ova are really much smaller than the diagram shows. An ovum is the size of a tiny speck of sand. You need a microscope to see sperm.

1 Where inside a woman are sperm deposited?

2 How do sperm reach the ovum?

3 Where inside a woman do the sperm and ovum meet?

The inside of the **uterus** has a thick lining ready to receive a fertilised ovum. If the ovum released each month does not meet a sperm, the lining is changed for a new one. The old lining breaks down and leaves the woman's body through her vagina. This is her monthly **period**.

4 Why do women have periods?

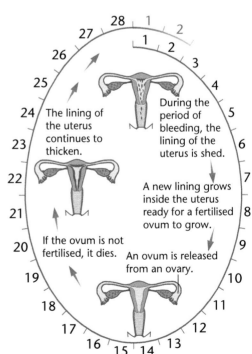

The lining of the uterus continues to thicken.

During the period of bleeding, the lining of the uterus is shed.

A new lining grows inside the uterus ready for a fertilised ovum to grow.

If the ovum is not fertilised, it dies.

An ovum is released from an ovary.

■ What happens to a fertilised ovum?

As the fertilised ovum travels down the oviduct to the uterus, it begins to grow. The first cell splits into two to form two cells. Then each of these cells splits, to make four cells altogether. This process continues, forming a ball of cells.

Inside the uterus, the ball of cells sinks into the thick, soft lining. We call this **implantation**.

The ball of cells changes shape as it grows, and forms a head, body, arms and legs. It is then called an <u>embryo</u>.

As the weeks go by and the embryo grows, it starts to look more and more human. We then call it a <u>fetus</u>.

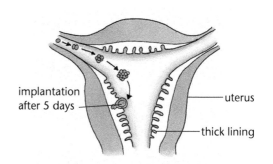

implantation after 5 days — uterus — thick lining

Time since fertilisation

4 weeks — embryo (1 cm) actual size

8 weeks — fetus (3 cm) $\frac{1}{2}$ size

12 weeks — fetus (12 cm) $\frac{1}{5}$ size

28 weeks — fetus (34 cm) $\frac{1}{10}$ size

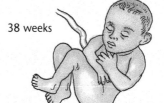

38 weeks — baby (52 cm) $\frac{1}{12}$ size

5 Put these sentences into the right order. The first one is in the correct place.

■ The fertilised ovum grows into a ball of cells.

■ The ball of cells grows into an embryo.

■ The embryo grows into a fetus.

■ The ball of cells attaches to the uterus.

6 Copy and complete the table.

Weeks since fertilisation	Size (cm)	What we call it
4		
8		
12		
38		

WHAT YOU NEED TO REMEMBER (Copy and complete using the **key words**)

The start of pregnancy

The _____ and ovum join in an _____. We call this _____.

The fertilised ovum divides as it travels down the oviduct to the uterus.
The ball of cells sinks into the lining of the _____. We call this _____.

If an ovum is not fertilised, the lining of the uterus breaks down and causes the bleeding called a monthly _____.

More about pregnancy and periods: CORE+ C1.12, C1.13

C1.6 New plants

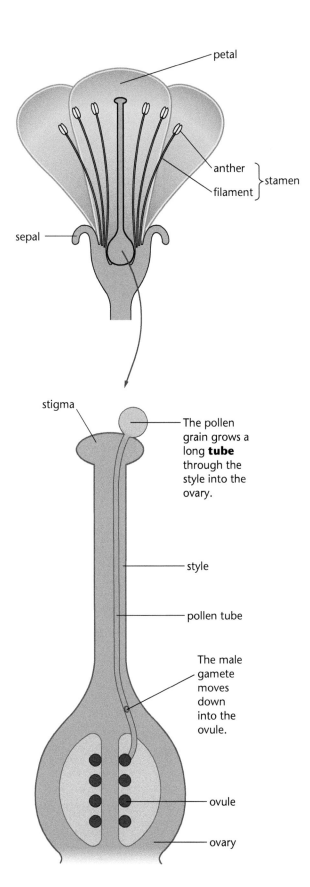

petal

anther ⎫
filament ⎭ stamen

sepal

For a flowering plant to reproduce, a female gamete (sex cell) in the plant must join with a male gamete (sex cell) from another plant.

The male gamete is in a pollen grain. Pollen from an **anther** of one flower must be moved to the **stigma** of another flower. We call this **pollination**. In some plants wind carries the pollen. In other plants the pollen is carried by insects or other small animals.

1 Copy and complete the sentences.

The pollen from one plant travels from its anther to the _____ of another plant.
This transfer of pollen is called _____.

stigma

The pollen grain grows a long **tube** through the style into the ovary.

▨ After pollination, what next?

When pollen has landed on a stigma, the male gamete must travel to the female gamete in an ovule. The diagram shows how this happens.

style

2 Put the sentences into the correct order to describe how the male gamete reaches the ovule. The first sentence is in the correct place.

Pollen grain lands on the stigma.

■ The male gamete moves down the pollen tube into the ovule.

■ The pollen tube grows down to an ovule.

■ The pollen tube reaches the ovary.

■ A pollen tube grows down through the style.

pollen tube

The male gamete moves down into the ovule.

ovule

ovary

▧ Inside the ovule

The male gamete travels down the **pollen** tube into the ovule.

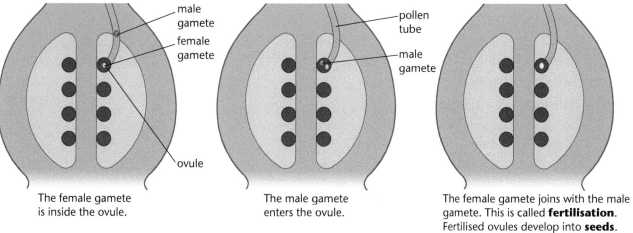

The female gamete is inside the ovule.

The male gamete enters the ovule.

The female gamete joins with the male gamete. This is called **fertilisation**. Fertilised ovules develop into **seeds**.

3 What happens when the male gamete enters the ovule?

4 What do we call this process?

▧ Wrong flower, wrong pollen

Pollen will not always land on another flower of the same type.

Some scientists did an experiment to find out whether pollen could fertilise ovules of a different type of plant. The diagram shows what happened.

5 (a) What did the scientists do?

(b) What did they find out?

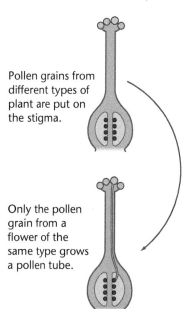

Pollen grains from different types of plant are put on the stigma.

Only the pollen grain from a flower of the same type grows a pollen tube.

WHAT YOU NEED TO REMEMBER (Copy and complete using the **key words**)

New plants

There are three steps to make a new plant.

1 Pollen is transferred from an _____ of one flower to the _____ of another flower of the same type. We call this _____.

2 A pollen _____ grows down through the style. The male gamete uses this to reach the female gamete.

3 The two gametes join together. The female gamete and the male gamete join to make one cell. We call this _____. Fertilised ovules develop into _____ inside a fruit.

More about pollination: CORE+ C1.14

Follows on from: 1.7, 1.8

C1.7 Classification

Scientists sort living things into groups. They put living things which have the same features into the same group. Grouping living things this way is called **classification**.

Scientists don't all agree about how to do this, but many scientists sort living things into five main groups or kingdoms. These are **plants**, **animals**, **fungi**, **monera** and **protoctists**.

1 What is classification?

These groups contain living things which can look very different. For example, mushrooms have caps, stalks and lots of underground threads, but yeast cells are microscopic. Scientists classify both of them as fungi because they have important features which are the same. Their cells have walls but they don't contain chloroplasts. So they cannot make their own food.

2 Copy and complete the table.

Group	Features	Examples
plants		
animals		
fungi		
monera		
protoctists		

Sometimes scientists group living things in a different way. For example, it can be useful to group together the living things which can only be seen with a microscope. Scientists call these micro-organisms or **microbes**.

3 Write down the names of three groups that have microbes in them.

Plants make their own food.

Animals must eat other living things.

Yeast (a unicellular fungus)

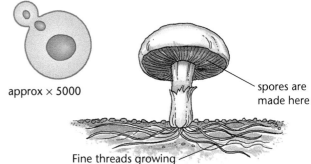

approx × 5000

spores are made here

Fine threads growing underground are the biggest part of the fungus.

Mushroom (a multicellular fungus)

magnified 20000 times

Bacteria are unicellular and microscopic. They don't have a proper nucleus so they belong to the monera.

Most protoctists are unicellular and microscopic. Some have features of animals. Others are more like plants.

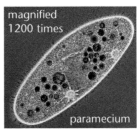

magnified 1200 times

paramecium

Classifying plants

There are lots of different kinds of plants, so it's useful to sort them into smaller groups. The key shows the four main groups.

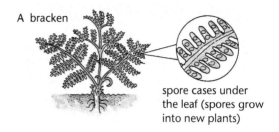

A bracken

spore cases under the leaf (spores grow into new plants)

Key

1 Plant makes seeds.	Go to 2.
Plant makes spores.	Go to 3.
2 Seeds are made in cones.	**conifers**
Seeds are made in flowers.	**flowering plants**
3 Plant has no proper roots.	**mosses** and **liverworts**
Plant has leaves, stems and roots.	**ferns**

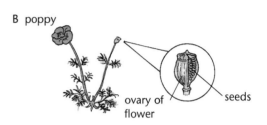

B poppy

ovary of flower

seeds

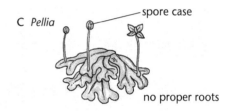

C *Pellia*

spore case

no proper roots

4 Copy the table. Use the key to find out which groups plants A, B, C and D belong to. Then complete your table.

Plant	Group
A bracken	
B poppy	
C *Pellia*	
D Scots pine	

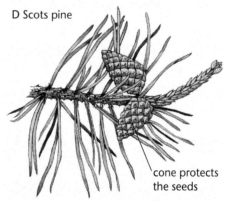

D Scots pine

cone protects the seeds

WHAT YOU NEED TO REMEMBER (Copy and complete using the **key words**)

Classification

Scientists usually sort living things into five main groups or kingdoms: _____, _____, _____, _____ and _____.
This is called _____.

It is sometimes useful to group microscopic living things as _____ .

There are four main groups of plants: f_____ p_____, c_____, f_____ and m_____ and l_____ .

More about classification: CORE+ C1.15, C1.16

Follows on from: 1.9, 1.10

C1.8 Groups of animals

All animals are alike in some ways. For example, they all get their food by eating something else.

But there are still plenty of differences between animals. This is why we split the different animals into smaller groups.

First we split them into two groups.

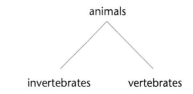
animals

invertebrates   vertebrates

This animal has a soft body.

backbone

1 Copy and complete the sentences.

Animals are split into _____ main groups.
Animals without a backbone are called _____.
If they have a backbone they are _____.

■ Invertebrates

Most kinds of animals do not have a backbone. They are <u>invertebrates</u>.

Invertebrates are usually fairly small, except for a few types that live in the sea.

The table below shows the five main groups of invertebrates. It also tells you the main features of each group.

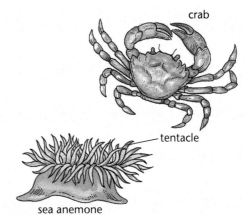
crab

tentacle

sea anemone

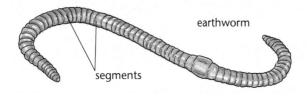
earthworm

segments

liver fluke

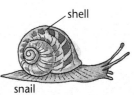
shell

snail

2 Copy the table and add the name of <u>one</u> example for each group.

Invertebrate group	Main features	Example
coelenterates	have tentacles and a bag-shaped body	
platyhelminths (flatworms)	have thin flat bodies	
annelid worms (true worms)	have soft segmented bodies	
molluscs	have soft bodies with a hard shell	
arthropods	have a hard outer skeleton and jointed limbs	

■ **Vertebrates**

We can also put vertebrates into different groups or
classes. These photographs show one example
from each group of vertebrates.

3 Copy the following diagram. Then use the information from the photographs to complete it.

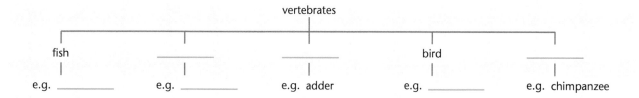

vertebrates

fish   _____   _____   bird   _____

e.g. _____   e.g. _____   e.g. adder   e.g. _____   e.g. chimpanzee

*Frogs have moist skin with no
scales. Their eggs have no
shells. They are amphibians.*

*The adder is a reptile. It has
a dry scaly skin and its eggs
have tough shells.*

*Goldfish have scales, gills
and fins. They have a
streamlined shape. Their
eggs have no shells.*

*Chimpanzees are mammals.
They have hair and feed their
young on milk.*

*The golden plover has feathers
and lays eggs with hard shells.*

WHAT YOU NEED TO REMEMBER

Groups of animals

*You need to be able to classify animals into their main groups, just as you have done in the questions
on this spread. Revise the groups of arthropods (page 29) and vertebrates (pages 26–27).*

Follows on from: 4.7, 4.8

C1.9 Variation

Different species of plants and animals look different. Even members of the same species are different in some ways. We say that they **vary**.

1 Look at the pictures. Write down <u>three</u> ways that tomatoes can be different from each other.

To grow yellow tomatoes, you need to plant seeds from other yellow tomatoes. This is because tomato colour is passed on from one generation to the next. We say it is **inherited**.

2 **(a)** Tomato T is from a plant bred from two yellow-fruited plants. If you plant seeds from this tomato, what colour tomatoes will you get?

   (b) Use the picture to help you to explain your answer.

■ Does inheritance cause all differences?

3 Look at the bunch of tomatoes in the diagram. Write down <u>one</u> reason why:

   (a) on August 4th, tomato A is bigger than tomato B;

   (b) when they are fully grown, A and B are the same size.

REMEMBER from page 65

To grow, plants need sunlight, water, carbon dioxide and minerals.

The two plum tomatoes in the photograph are both fully grown. They are different from each other because they grew in different conditions. We say that the **environment** caused the difference.

4 Write down <u>two</u> differences in the environment which could have made one tomato grow bigger than the other.

REMEMBER from page 83

A <u>species</u> is one kind of living thing. It is different from other species and cannot interbreed with them.

Tomatoes vary.

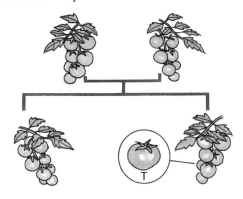

tomatoes on August 4th

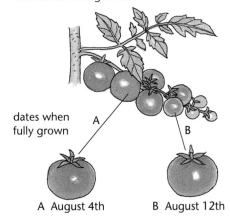

dates when fully grown

A August 4th   B August 12th

Plum tomatoes.

Inheritance or environment?

Sandy grew some plants using the seeds from one lupin plant. She measured their heights. They were all different. She put them into groups in a table.

Height of plants (cm)	Tally	Total
41–50	I	1
51–60	III	3
61–70	₦ I	6
71–80	IIII	4
81–90	II	2

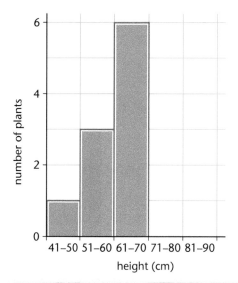

5 Copy and complete the bar chart of Sandy's results.

6 Look at the flowers. Sandy collected one from each plant. Copy and complete the table.

Colour	Tally	Total
blue	₦ IIII	9

Differences between plants or animals of the same species can be caused by:

- inheritance;
- the environment;
- a **mixture** of inheritance and environment.

7 Read the information in the box. Then explain, as fully as you can, why Sandy's plants differed in:

(a) size;

(b) flower colour.

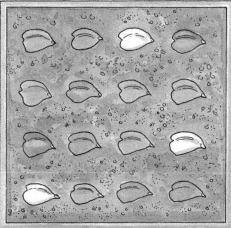

DID YOU KNOW?

The embryo plant in a lupin seed is made from two sex cells. The colour of a lupin, and how big it <u>can</u> grow, are both inherited from the parent plants. How big a lupin <u>actually</u> grows also depends on its environment.

WHAT YOU NEED TO REMEMBER (Copy and complete using the **key words**)

Variation

Members of a species _____. Some of the differences between them are passed on from their parents. We say that these differences are _____.

The _____ also causes differences. These differences are not passed on.

A _____ of inheritance and environment causes other differences.

More about inheritance and environment: CORE+ C1.17, C2.17

C1.10 Specialised cells

Your body has many different types of cell. Each of them has the right features to do a particular job. We say that each cell is <u>specialised</u> to do its job.

Different animal cells

The air you breathe in contains tiny particles of dust and microbes. These could damage your lungs.

1 (a) Which cells in your nose help your body to overcome this problem?

(b) Explain how these cells do their job.

At the start of reproduction, sperm and ova join together to develop into a new animal. Male animals make sperm cells. These must reach the female ova if they are to **fertilise** them.

2 Describe how sperm cells and ova are adapted to make reproduction successful.

Different plant cells

Palisade cells are found inside the leaves of plants.

The diagram shows the special structures that these cells have.

3 (a) What special structures do plant palisade cells have?

(b) How do these help them to do their job?

Plants also need water to live. Their roots take in water from the soil.

4 Explain in as much detail as you can how root hair cells are adapted to do their job.

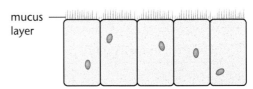

These hairs (cilia) move particles to the back of the throat. The particles are swallowed and then destroyed by stomach acid.

mucus layer

Ciliated epithelium cells line your nose.

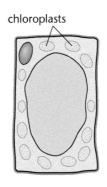

The nucleus of each cell contains the genetic material.

Sperm has a tail so that it can swim to the egg.

Cytoplasm contains food for the embryo so that it can start to grow.

Sperm and egg cells.

chloroplasts

Palisade cells have chloroplasts. They contain chlorophyll which traps light energy. The cell uses light to make food.

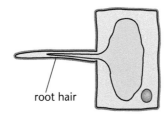

root hair

Root cells have tiny hairs to increase the root's surface area. This helps the root take in water.

WHAT YOU NEED TO REMEMBER

Specialised cells

You will need to be able to recognise specialised animal and plant cells like those on this page, and explain how each cell is specialised to do its job. See also pages 68, 69, 107, 108, 109 and 148.

C1.11 Organ systems

■ Your organs carry out the processes of life. For example, a woman's vagina, ovaries, oviducts and uterus are all involved in reproduction. These four organs share the work so that reproduction can happen. They are an **organ system**.

REMEMBER from page 108

Groups of similar cells are called <u>tissues</u>. Different tissues join together to make an <u>organ</u>.

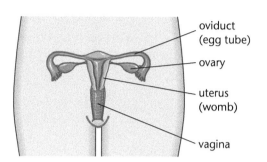

1 The female reproductive system in plants has the same job as in animals but it has a different design. Copy and complete the table.

Job	Animal organ	Plant organ
makes the female gamete	ovary	
sperm or pollen is put here	vagina	
sperm or male gamete travels along here to meet the female gamete	oviduct	
fertilised ovum develops here	uterus	

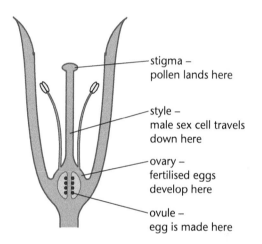

■ The cells in your body produce waste substances. These waste substances are poisonous so your body has to get rid of them. We say that they have to be <u>excreted</u>.

One of these waste products is <u>urea</u>. Several organs work together to get rid of urea. The diagram shows the organs that make up this system.

2 Use the information from the diagram to complete a flow chart that shows what happens to urea in your body. The first line is done for you.

Liver cells make urea and pass it into the blood.

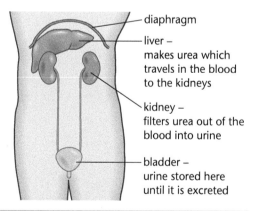

WHAT YOU NEED TO REMEMBER (Copy and complete using the **key words**)

Organ systems

Organs work together as _____ _____. They enable life processes to take place.

See also: respiratory system (page 35), skeletal system (page 46), circulatory, nervous and digestive systems (page 16).

C1.12 Pregnancy and birth

■ Feeding the fetus

As a fetus grows inside the uterus, so does a special organ called the **placenta**. The placenta lets blood from the mother and blood from the fetus come very close to each other without actually mixing. The fetus is inside a bag of fluid called the amniotic fluid.

1 Where is the placenta?

2 What connects the placenta to the fetus?

3 **(a)** What <u>two</u> substances pass from the mother to the fetus across the placenta?

   (b) What <u>two</u> substances pass from the fetus to the mother?

■ Birth

When the baby is ready to be born, the uterus muscles start to **contract**. This is called <u>labour</u>. Gradually the contractions get stronger, more often and more painful. The mother also contracts her abdomen muscles to help push the baby out.

Finally the baby is born, usually head first, through the vagina. The umbilical cord is cut. About 15 minutes later the placenta and the bag that held the fluid are pushed out. We call these the <u>afterbirth</u>.

4 Write down <u>two</u> different sets of muscles that contract to push the baby out.

5 Why is the umbilical cord tied before it is cut?

6 What is the afterbirth?

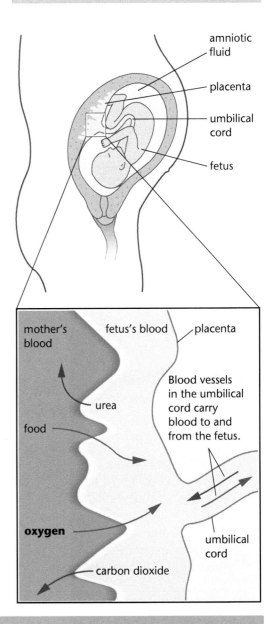

amniotic fluid

placenta

umbilical cord

fetus

mother's blood

fetus's blood

placenta

urea

food

Blood vessels in the umbilical cord carry blood to and from the fetus.

oxygen

umbilical cord

carbon dioxide

WHAT YOU NEED TO REMEMBER (Copy and complete using the **key words**)

Pregnancy and birth

When an embryo embeds itself in the uterus lining, a special organ called the _____ forms.
Nutrients and _____ pass from the mother to the fetus.
Waste from the _____ passes into the mother's blood.

After about 38 weeks, the uterus muscles _____ to push the baby out.
The placenta is no longer needed so it is also pushed out.

C1.13 The menstrual cycle

A woman can release hundreds of ova (eggs) during her life. Most of these are never fertilised.

About once a month, an **ovary** releases an ovum. Each month the **uterus** lining thickens so it is ready for an embryo to grow.

If the ovum is not fertilised, the lining is not needed. It breaks down and passes out of the body with a little blood. A new lining then starts to grow and the cycle starts over again. We call this the menstrual cycle.

1 Why does the uterus lining thicken?

2 What day in the cycle is an ovum released?

3 How long does a period usually last?

The cycle is controlled by hormones from the **ovaries** and the **pituitary** gland in the brain. One of the pituitary hormones makes an ovary release an ovum.

4 Which other hormone peaks when an ovum is released?

5 Many women feel tense just before their period. What might cause this?

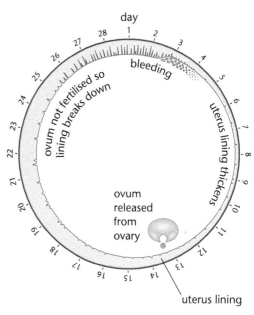

The menstrual cycle. Days are numbered from the first day of bleeding.

Hormones also affect how a woman feels at different times in the cycle.

Changes in the amounts of two hormones from the ovaries during the menstrual cycle.

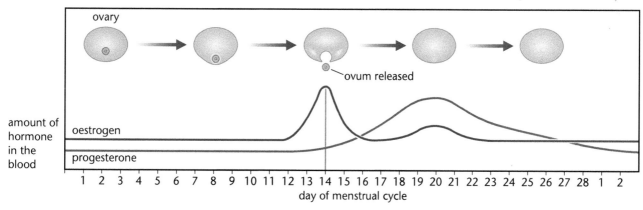

WHAT YOU NEED TO REMEMBER (Copy and complete using the **key words**)

The menstrual cycle

The menstrual cycle is a way of making sure that the lining of the _____ is ready for the implantation of an embryo each time an _____ releases an ovum (egg).
The menstrual cycle is controlled by _____ from the _____ and the _____ gland.

C1.14 Moving pollen and seeds

Flowering plants can't move from place to place. So, they need help to complete their life cycles.

1 Look at the diagram. Then copy and complete the table.

Part of plant moved	Process

These parts are moved by animals, wind or water. Plants are adapted to make sure that they are moved.

Adaptations for pollination

Animals such as **insects**, birds and bats are attracted to flowers for food. They pollinate them by accident. The design of flowers makes this accident likely to happen. Wind-pollinated flowers have a different design.

2 Look at the diagrams. Write down three adaptations for wind pollination and three adaptations for insect pollination.

Adaptations for dispersal of fruits and seeds

Seeds and fruits are **spread** by
- **wind**,
- sticking to fur or feathers,
- being eaten but not digested.

3 Match the seeds in the pictures with two of the ways that seeds are spread. Explain your answers.

 Find out some more examples of adaptations for dispersal.

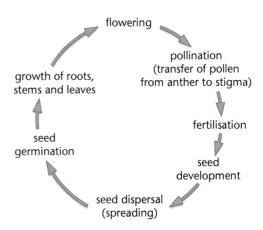

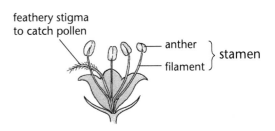

Small petals let the wind reach the anthers and stigma.

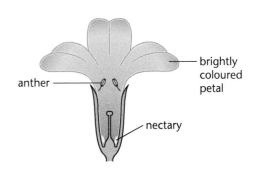

Some insects eat nectar or pollen. Scent and colour help them to find the flowers.

dandelion   burdock

WHAT YOU NEED TO REMEMBER (Copy and complete using the **key words**)

Some flowers are adapted to attract _____. Others have flowers that let the wind reach the anthers and stigmas.

Seeds are adapted to be dispersed or _____ by animals or the _____.

C1.15 Changing classifications

People have not always **classified** things in the same way.

A very famous Greek scientist called Aristotle lived from 384–322 BC. He wrote down ideas of grouping living things into two sets of plants and animals.

1 What features did Aristotle use to separate plants from animals?

2 How did he split the animal group up into smaller groups?

An Italian doctor called Andrea Cesalpino (1519–1603) used differences in reproductive parts to split plants into smaller groups. The Swedish botanist Linnaeus (1707–1778) made a more complete classification of plants and animals. Many improvements have since been made to his system.

3 How do we use plant reproduction to help us classify plants?

The **microscope** was invented at the beginning of the 16th century. Scientists saw microbes for the first time.

These organisms could not be grouped as plants or animals, because some had features of both groups! In 1861 John Hogg called microbes the third main group of living things.

4 Why can *Euglena* not be classified using Aristotle's system?

Charles Darwin (1809–1882) studied how living things developed from earlier simple organisms over millions of years. This is called **evolution**. Darwin showed that when you know which plants or animals are related to one another, it is easier to classify them. But when scientists group living things into families, they don't all agree. Now scientists are studying the **genes** of living things to find out which ones are related to each other.

5 Some scientists have suggested a new system for classifying plants. On what evidence have they based the new system?

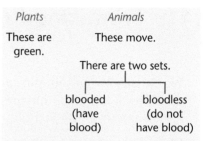

Plants — These are green.
Animals — These move. There are two sets.

blooded (have blood) — bloodless (do not have blood)

Aristotle's system of classification.

Ferns, mosses and liverworts produce spores.

Conifers and flowering plants produce seeds.

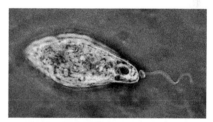

Euglena *is green and it moves.*

Scientists put roses and nettles in different families. Their genes show that they are related.

WHAT YOU NEED TO REMEMBER (Copy and complete using the **key words**)

Changing classifications

Living things have not always been _____ in the same way.
Scientists have gathered new information using scientific instruments like the _____.
They have also used new ideas from the study of _____ and of _____.

C1.16 From kingdom to species

We **classify** living things into five kingdoms. We then divide each kingdom into groups, and each of these groups into even smaller groups.

We classify rabbits as:

Kingdom	Animal
Phylum	Chordates (vertebrates)
Class	Mammals
Order	Lagomorpha
Family	Leporidae
Genus	*Oryctolagus*
Species	*cuniculus*

Animals in the same phylum, class or order are similar in some ways. Animals in the same family are even more alike. They are more closely related.

1 Look at the pictures. Why do scientists put rabbits and hares in the same family?

Species have different <u>common</u> names in different places. So, we give each species a **scientific** name made up of the names of its <u>genus</u> and its <u>species</u>. Scientists everywhere use these names. The scientific name for rabbits is *Oryctolagus cuniculus*.

2 We classify brown hares into the same groups as rabbits until we get to the genus and species. The scientific name for brown hares is *Lepus capensis*.

Write a list, like the one for rabbits, of the groups that brown hares belong to.

3 (a) Write down the scientific name for humans.

(b) Why are scientific names useful?

REMEMBER from page 83

A **species** is one kind of living thing. It is different from other species and cannot interbreed with them.

Common names:
English: rabbit
French: lapin
German: Kaninchen
Scientific name: *Oryctolagus cuniculus*

Common names:
English: brown hare
French: lièvre
German: Hase
Scientific name: *Lepus capensis*

The scientific name for humans is *Homo sapiens*.

WHAT YOU NEED TO REMEMBER (Copy and complete using the **key words**)

We _____ living things into groups, then each group into smaller groups. The smallest group is a _____. We give each species a _____ name with two parts.

C1.17 Champion leeks

Edward grew these leeks from one packet of seeds.

1 (a) Write down <u>two</u> ways that the leeks vary.

(b) Write down <u>two</u> possible reasons why they vary.

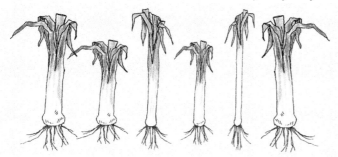

Sarah and Ben give the leeks fertiliser and water. They take out the weeds to give the leeks space and light.

■ Growing better leeks

Sarah and Ben enter their leeks in shows every year. They keep trying to grow the biggest and best leeks.

The environment affects how well leeks grow, so Sarah and Ben make sure they give the plants all that they need.

2 Look at the pictures. Write a list of the things Sarah and Ben do to make the plants grow well.

Even though they give all the leeks all the things they need, the plants still vary.

Sarah and Ben don't buy new packets of seeds every year. They **choose** their biggest and best plants and **breed** from them.

3 Look at the pictures. Describe how Sarah and Ben get their seeds.

We breed plants and animals with the characteristics we want. We call this **selective breeding**.

Sarah and Ben let these flower and pollinate each other.

They eat these.

↓

They collect the seeds.

↓

They grow next year's plants from these seeds.

WHAT YOU NEED TO REMEMBER (Copy and complete using the **key words**)

Champion leeks

We can _____ the plants and animals which best suit our needs.
We can _____ from them so they pass on their useful characteristics.
We call this _____ _____.

C2.1 Illness and health

Good health means feeling well in body and mind. There are many reasons for illness.

You can breathe in flu viruses.

Salmonella bacteria can get into your body through your food.

Microbes cause some diseases

Microbes are very small living things. You need a microscope to see them. Viruses, bacteria and some fungi are microbes. Some microbes can get inside your body and give you a disease. You can catch these diseases from other people.

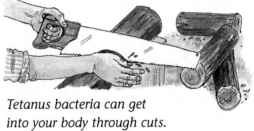

Tetanus bacteria can get into your body through cuts.

1 Write down <u>three</u> ways that microbes can get into your body.

You can be born with some diseases

Some diseases are **inherited** from your parents. You don't <u>catch</u> these diseases, you are <u>born</u> with them. Nobody else can catch inherited diseases from you. But you can pass them on to your own children.

2 (a) What is sickle-cell anaemia?

(b) Can you catch sickle-cell anaemia from someone who has it? Give a reason for your answer.

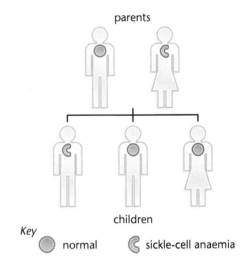

Sickle-cell anaemia is an illness that people can inherit from their parents. Their red blood cells are the wrong shape and do not carry oxygen very well.

Cells can go wrong

Your body makes new cells all the time. New cells are made when a cell divides in two. If cells divide too quickly, they go out of control and a tumour grows. We call this <u>cancer</u>. Ultraviolet rays and tar in cigarettes can cause cancer.

3 Why is it important that sun cream has UV (ultraviolet) protection?

4 Could someone with skin cancer pass it on to you?

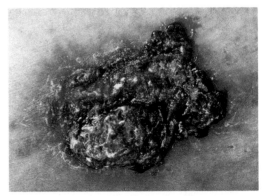

Ultraviolet rays from the Sun can cause skin cancer.

A poor diet can make you ill

It is important to eat the right sorts of foods in the right amounts to stay healthy. Too much food can make you overweight and put a strain on your heart. Just one mineral or **vitamin** missing from your diet can make you ill.

5 Copy and complete this table.

Illness	Cause of illness
heart disease	
	not enough iron
	too much sugar
weak bones	
poor sight in dim light	

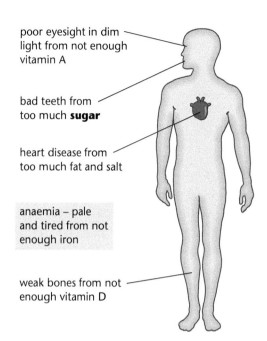

poor eyesight in dim light from not enough vitamin A

bad teeth from too much **sugar**

heart disease from too much fat and salt

anaemia – pale and tired from not enough iron

weak bones from not enough vitamin D

Some examples of problems caused by a poor diet.

Stress

Even if you eat the right foods and don't catch or inherit a disease, you can still be ill. Your mind needs to feel well too, but for many people the pressures and tensions of their lives cause stress. Stress can give you headaches, stomach ulcers and high blood pressure. You can help reduce stress by taking more time to exercise, relax and sleep.

6 Some doctors say that keeping a pet can reduce stress. Why do you think this is?

WHAT YOU NEED TO REMEMBER (Copy and complete using the **key words**)

Illness and health

You need to look after your body.

Some _____, such as viruses, fungi and bacteria, can make you ill.

Lack of just one mineral or _____ in your diet can cause a disease.
Too much fat, salt or _____ can harm you.

Some illnesses are passed on from parents to their children; we say that they are _____.

More about microbes: CORE+ C2.9, C2.10

Follows on from: 2.7, 2.8

C2.2 Some chemicals can damage your body

■ Smoking

The job of your lungs is to get oxygen into your blood and carbon dioxide out of your body. We call this <u>gas exchange</u>.

Cigarette smoke contains a poison called carbon monoxide. Some of this carbon monoxide is carried in your blood instead of oxygen. So your heart and lungs have to work harder to get the oxygen you need. This is why smokers get out of breath easily. In larger amounts, carbon monoxide can kill you.

1 Most athletes don't smoke. Why is this?

2 How does a smoker's lung look different from a non-smoker's lung?

The chemicals in cigarette smoke can also cause lung cancer and heart disease.

■ Alcohol

Alcohol is a poison. When you drink alcohol, your liver works hard to get rid of it. Your liver breaks the alcohol down into carbon dioxide and water. Too much alcohol damages your liver.

Alcohol also slows your brain down. People who have been drinking are clumsy and slow to react.

3 Which organ removes alcohol from your body?

4 **(a)** Look at the table. Jordan had two pints of beer. How long did it take his body to get rid of all the alcohol?

(b) How much does the amount of alcohol in Jordan's blood go down each hour?

(c) If Jordan drank only one pint of beer, how long would it take his body to remove the alcohol?

REMEMBER from page 36

All the cells in your body need oxygen. They get this from your blood.

Non-smoker's lung.

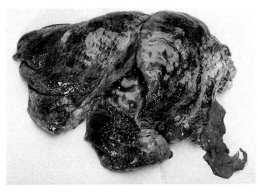

Smoker's lung.

This table shows the amount of alcohol in Jordan's blood after he drank two pints of beer.

Time (hours)	Amount of alcohol in the blood (grams per litre)
0	8
1	6
2	4
3	2
4	0
5	0

Medicines

Medicines are drugs you take when you are ill to help you feel better. For example, you take drugs like aspirin or paracetamol for a headache.

5 Why is it dangerous to take more aspirin or paracetamol than you should?

Antibiotics are drugs that kill bacteria. You can take antibiotics for a sore throat. It is important to take all of the antibiotics the doctor gives you.

6 What happens if you stop taking antibiotics too early?

 Find out the names of some antibiotics. What are the differences between antibiotics, antiseptics and disinfectants?

Illegal drugs

Some people take drugs like ecstasy, LSD and cannabis or sniff solvents to feel different. All these drugs **damage** your body and when the effects wear off you can feel worse than you did before.

Some people who are training to be athletes may be offered illegal drugs called steroids which help them build muscle quickly. Steroids have side effects such as mood changes and heart damage.

7 (a) Write down two different reasons why people might want to take illegal drugs.

(b) In each case, write down two reasons why taking illegal drugs isn't a good idea.

WARNING

Never take a bigger dose of a medicine than it says on the packet. Too much aspirin can damage your stomach. Too much paracetamol can damage your liver. An overdose of these drugs can kill you.

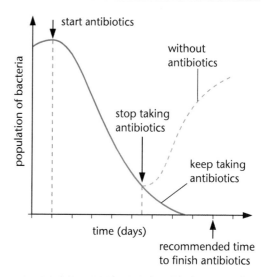

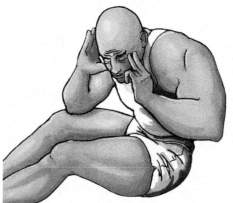

Athletes caught taking steroids to improve their performance are banned from competitions.

WHAT YOU NEED TO REMEMBER (Copy and complete using the **key words**)

Some chemicals can damage your body

Drugs that can help your body if you use them properly are called _____.

Smoking, alcohol, solvents and other drugs _____ your body.

More about antibiotics: CORE+ C2.10   More about smoking: CORE+ C2.11

Follows on from: 2.1, 3.3, 3.4

C2.3 Healthy eating

To stay **healthy** you need to eat the right sorts of foods in the right amounts. We call this a <u>balanced diet</u>.

REMEMBER from pages 54–57

The food you eat must contain:
- **carbohydrates** and **fats** for energy;
- **proteins** for growth;
- **fibre** to stop you getting constipated;
- small amounts of **vitamins** and **minerals**.

You must also drink plenty of water.

Dishes of the world

People around the world can get a healthy diet from all sorts of different foods.

What you need	Foods you can get them from
carbohydrates (starch and sugar)	rice, potatoes, noodles, chapatis, bread, maize, pasta
fats	oil, dairy foods, meat
proteins	fish, prawns, lentils, peas, meat
fibre	lentils, vegetables

West Indian dish: fish and rice.

1 **(a)** Write down <u>one</u> food which is a good source of protein in the West Indian dish.

   (b) Write down <u>one</u> food which is a good source of fibre in the Indian dish.

   (c) Write down <u>one</u> food which is a good source of carbohydrate in the Chinese dish.

Indian dish: dahl (made from lentils) and chapatis.

Staple foods

<u>Staple</u> foods contain a lot of carbohydrate as starch. They make up a large part of people's diets. In Britain the staple foods are wheat (bread) and potato, in India one of the staple foods is rice and in parts of Africa it is maize.

2 Copy and complete the sentences.

Staple foods contain mainly _____
(as _____).
You need this in your diet for _____ .

Chinese dish: prawn stir-fry and noodles.

A problem with maize

Children need more than just staple foods to be healthy.

Maya lives in Africa. She is weak and ill. Her skin cracks easily and her liver is damaged. She has an illness called kwashiorkor and she will probably die before she is five years old. Maya's family is poor, so she eats maize for most of her meals.

3 Write down <u>two</u> reasons why a diet of just maize is unhealthy.

4 Why do children need to eat protein?

5 Look at the picture of Maya and write down <u>two</u> things you can see wrong with her.

Maya's baby brother is healthy. He feeds on his mother's breast milk. Milk contains all the protein and vitamins that a young child needs.

6 If Maya can get the right food, she will get better within a month. Write down <u>one</u> food she could eat to give her more protein.

Maize is often called corn-on-the-cob. Where maize is the staple food, many children don't get all the protein and vitamins they need.

Maya has kwashiorkor

after one month's treatment

Other diets can also be a problem

Many people get enough to eat but they eat too much of some things and not enough of others. We say their diets are not balanced. A lot of people in Britain have bad teeth from eating too much sugar. A few people have an illness called scurvy from not eating enough fresh fruit.

7 Look at the picture. If you eat meals like this all the time you will not be very healthy. Write down <u>two</u> reasons why.

WHAT YOU NEED TO REMEMBER (Copy and complete using the **key words**)

Healthy eating

You need to eat a variety of food to stay _____. The important things in your diet are
c_____, f_____, p_____, f_____, v_____, m_____ and water.

More about vitamins: CORE+ C2.12

C2.4 Digesting your food

REMEMBER from page 61

Only small **soluble** molecules can pass into your blood to be carried to your cells. This means that the food you eat has to be broken down.

Your teeth grind up your food.

Saliva makes food soft and slippery so that you can swallow it easily. Then muscles push the food along the oesophagus (gullet) to your stomach.

Glands add digestive juices to the food. These contain **enzymes** that break down large food molecules into smaller ones. This is **digestion**.

Digested food passes from your small **intestine** into your blood. This is absorption.

1 Your friends think that chewing food makes it small enough to be absorbed into your blood. Explain why this is not true.

2 Copy and complete the sentences.

Even small pieces of food contain large _____. Digestive juices contain _____ which break these down.

Different kinds of enzymes

A balanced meal contains different types of foods. Different enzymes digest each different type of food.

3 Copy the table. Use the diagram to help you to complete the table.

Gland	What its enzymes digest
salivary glands	_____
stomach lining	_____
_____	no enzymes, but juice splits fats into tiny drops
pancreas	_____, _____, _____
small intestine lining	_____, _____, _____

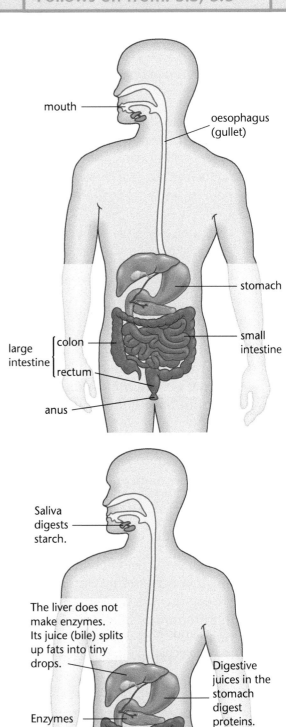

mouth

oesophagus (gullet)

stomach

small intestine

large intestine { colon

{ rectum

anus

Saliva digests starch.

The liver does not make enzymes. Its juice (bile) splits up fats into tiny drops.

Digestive juices in the stomach digest proteins.

Enzymes from the **pancreas** go into the small intestine. They digest starch, proteins and fats.

Enzymes from the small intestine lining digest sugars, proteins and fats.

What are different foods digested into?

The food you eat is a mixture of large molecules. The diagram shows what these molecules are. It also shows the smaller molecules that are produced when the large molecules are digested.

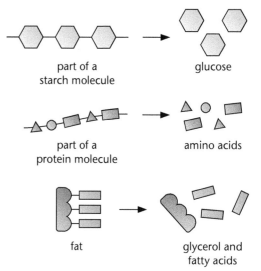

part of a
starch molecule

glucose

part of a
protein molecule

amino acids

fat

glycerol and
fatty acids

4 Copy and complete a table, using the headings shown, to show what happens to starch, protein and fats.

Large molecules ...	... are digested into these small molecules

What happens where?

Different parts of the digestive system have different jobs.

5 Put these sentences into the correct order. Use the diagram on page 138 to help you do this. You don't need to write out the sentences, just use the letters A to F.

A   Muscles in the stomach wall churn up food. The lining makes digestive juices.

B   Solid waste called faeces leaves the anus. We say that it is egested. Most of this waste is fibre that we cannot digest. It helps to keep the intestine healthy because it gives muscles in the intestine wall something to push on to move the food along.

C   Muscles in the oesophagus (gullet) wall squeeze food along. There are muscles like these all the way through the digestive system.

D   In the mouth, teeth grind the food into small pieces. Salivary glands make saliva. This wets the food so it can be easily swallowed. Saliva also starts to digest some of the food.

E   Glands in the small intestine lining add digestive juices to the food. Small digested food molecules are absorbed into the blood.

F   Water is absorbed from part of the large intestine called the colon.

WHAT YOU NEED TO REMEMBER (Copy and complete using the **key words**)

Digesting your food

Large food molecules are broken down by _____._____ in digestive juices. We call this _____.

Digestive juices are made in your salivary _____, stomach lining, _____ and small intestine lining.

You absorb small, _____ molecules of food in your small _____.

More about enzymes: CORE+ C2.13

Follows on from: 3.7

C2.5 Using your food

REMEMBER from page 62

Food gives you **energy** for moving, growing and keeping warm.

Food also gives you **materials** for making new cells.

Food to make new cells

Like all living things, you are made of cells. To stay healthy, you need to make new cells all the time.

Young people need new cells to grow. Even adults need new cells.

1 Look at the picture. Write down <u>two</u> reasons why adults need to produce new cells.

2 Where do you get the proteins and other materials you need to make new cells?

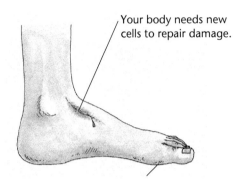

Your body needs new cells to repair damage.

Skin cells have to be replaced as they get worn away.

Cells need energy too

Cells get the energy they need from food. Food that is used by your cells for energy is your body's fuel.

3 Look at the diagram, then copy and complete the sentences.

The energy which cells need comes from a fuel called _____. Cells need _____ to make the glucose give up its energy.

When cells release energy from glucose, we say they **respire**.

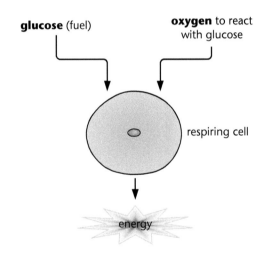

glucose (fuel)

oxygen to react with glucose

respiring cell

energy

How your cells get glucose

You don't eat much glucose. Your digestive system digests substances such as starch to produce the glucose that your cells need.

Enzymes break starch down into small glucose molecules in your digestive system.

You absorb the small glucose molecules into your blood system.

Your **blood** transports them around your body.

They pass into your **cells** so that your cells can use them.

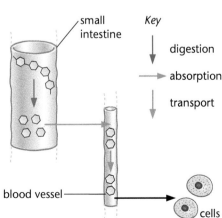

small intestine

Key

digestion

absorption

transport

blood vessel

cells

4 Copy and complete the flow chart by writing the following ideas in the correct order.

- used by your cells to provide energy

- absorbed into your blood

- digested by enzymes into glucose

- transported to your body cells

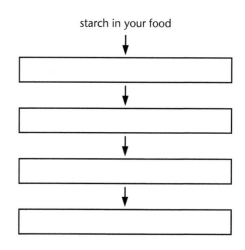

starch in your food

Cells make waste

Cells release waste when they respire.

5 Look at the diagram on the right, and the one in the middle of the opposite page. Then copy and complete this table.

Respiring cells	
take in	release

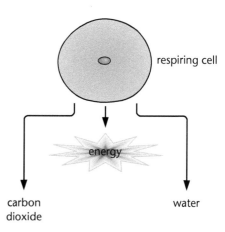

respiring cell

energy

carbon dioxide

water

Carbon dioxide waste is poisonous. To stay healthy, you have to get rid of it. You breathe it out. We say that your lungs excrete it.

WHAT YOU NEED TO REMEMBER (Copy and complete using the **key words**)

Using your food

Molecules of glucose from digested food travel in your _____ to all the _____ in your body. Cells break down the _____ to release _____.
We say they _____. They need _____ to do this.

Your food also supplies cells with the _____ they need to make new cells and to repair or replace damaged ones.

Note: All living cells, including plant cells, respire.

More about respiration: CORE+ C3.11

141

Follows on from: 2.4, 2.5

C2.6 What happens when you exercise?

When you **exercise**, your muscles work harder. Your muscle cells need to release more energy so they respire faster. Some of the energy released by respiration makes you warmer. So your body becomes hotter when you exercise.

REMEMBER from page 39

The cells of your muscles need oxygen and glucose to produce energy. Cells make carbon dioxide and other waste which the blood carries away.

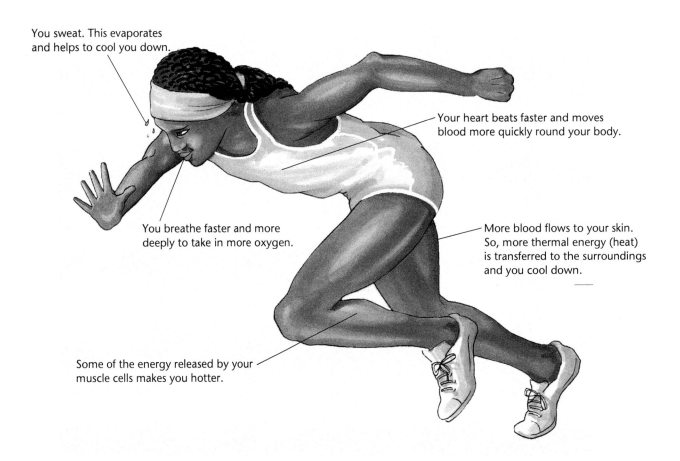

You sweat. This evaporates and helps to cool you down.

Your heart beats faster and moves blood more quickly round your body.

You breathe faster and more deeply to take in more oxygen.

More blood flows to your skin. So, more thermal energy (heat) is transferred to the surroundings and you cool down.

Some of the energy released by your muscle cells makes you hotter.

1 When you exercise, how do you get more oxygen into your body and then get it to your cells more quickly?

2 (a) Why do you feel hot when you exercise?

(b) What does your body do to cool you down?

(c) If athletes don't put a tracksuit on after a race, they get cold. Explain this as fully as you can.

How do you get the energy to exercise?

3 Copy and complete the sentences. Use the diagram to help you.

In muscles, _____ and glucose pass out of the blood and into the cells. The cells break down glucose using oxygen to release _____.
We call this _____.

A waste product called _____ _____ is produced. Blood carries this to the _____ where it is breathed out.

You **breathe** air in and out.

Cells in your muscles use oxygen and glucose to get energy. This process is called **respiration**.
Carbon dioxide is a waste product

Your blood **transports** oxygen and glucose to your muscles and carries carbon dioxide away

Gases go into and out of your body in your lungs. Oxygen goes into the blood and carbon dioxide goes into the air. We say that your lungs **exchange** gases.

WHAT YOU NEED TO REMEMBER (Copy and complete using the **key words**)

What happens when you exercise?

These are the things that must happen so your muscle cells can release energy when you exercise:

■ You _____ air in and out of your lungs.

■ In gas _____ in your lungs, oxygen goes into the blood and carbon dioxide goes out.

■ Your blood _____ glucose and oxygen to your muscle cells.

■ Cells break down glucose to release energy. This is _____.

All these things go on more quickly when you _____.

You need to be able to label a diagram of the respiratory system (page 36).

More about exercise: CORE+ C2.14

Follows on from: 2.2, 2.3

C2.7 Keeping fit

Exercise helps you feel good in mind and body. It helps you control your weight, and strengthens your muscles, heart and bones. It can be good fun too.

1 Write down <u>four</u> good reasons why everyone needs to exercise.

Improving your circulation

The flow of blood around your body is called your <u>circulation</u>. Your heart gets stronger and your blood circulation improves as you train.

2 Use the diagram to help you put these sentences about circulation into the right order. The first sentence is in the correct place.

> Your heart pumps blood to your body cells.

- Blood collects oxygen and gets rid of carbon dioxide.

- Blood from body cells returns to the right side of your heart in veins.

- Blood leaves your lungs in veins to go back to the left side of your heart.

- Your heart pumps blood in arteries to your lungs.

- Body cells take oxygen from the blood and put carbon dioxide in.

3 In one circuit round the body, how many times does blood go through your heart?

Capillaries are the smallest blood vessels in your body. They carry the blood between arteries and veins. There are millions of tiny capillaries all over your body bringing blood close to every cell.

4 Why do you need capillaries?

REMEMBER from page 35

Your **heart** pumps blood around your body. It pumps more quickly when you exercise.

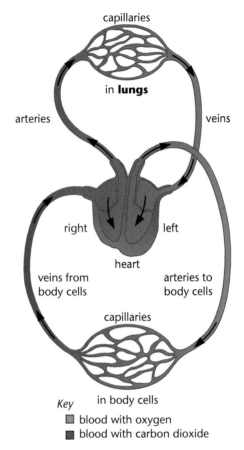

Key
- blood with oxygen
- blood with carbon dioxide

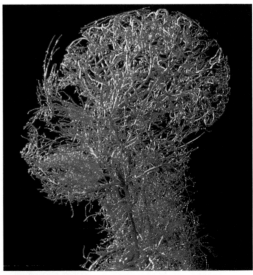

Capillary walls are thin. **Oxygen** *and* **glucose** *pass from the blood to the cells.* **Carbon dioxide** *passes into the blood.*

Getting started with exercise

If you are not very active now, you must build up slowly. Aim to exercise for at least 30 minutes three times a week. The more you exercise, the fitter you will become. Different types of exercise use different muscles so try to do more than one type of exercise.

5 Why is swimming good for you?

6 Why do rugby players get a lot of joint injuries?

7 What advantages does aerobics have over cycling as a form of exercise?

Team games, such as rugby and hockey, are good for stamina and strength. Sudden stops and turns may damage ankles and knees.

Swimming is a great way to get fit, especially if you are overweight. There is less stress on your joints because the water supports you.

Cycling is good for leg strength and stamina (being able to keep going). Always wear a cycle helmet.

Exercise classes (dance and aerobics) give you an all-over workout.

WHAT YOU NEED TO REMEMBER (Copy and complete using the **key words**)

Keeping fit

Your _____ pumps blood around your body.

Blood carries _____ and _____ to cells and takes away _____ _____ and other waste.

You need to be able to label a diagram of your heart and circulation and to know the features of arteries, veins and capillaries (page 34).

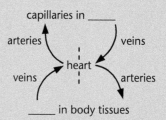

More about gas exchange: CORE+ C2.15   More about capillaries: CORE+ C2.16

Follows on from: 2.9, 2.10

C2.8 Take care when you exercise

Look at the pictures. These athletes are doing warm-up exercises in which they are gently stretching their muscles. If they do this, they are less likely to strain a muscle.

1 Why should you warm up before you play a sport?

But even when you have warmed up, you can sometimes injure muscles and joints.

Athletes do warm-up exercises before a race.

▪ Sprains

Omar has twisted his ankle playing football. He has injured one of the **joints** between the bones; we call this a <u>sprain</u>. The ligament that holds his ankle joint in place has been over-stretched. It hurts and Omar can't stand on that foot. Luckily his friend Baljeet has learnt first aid.

2 What is a sprain?

3 Why did Baljeet put a wet cold towel on Omar's ankle?

Later, Baljeet bandaged the ankle firmly.

4 Why do you think it is important not to tie the bandage too tight?

Omar needs to rest his ankle for a few days and not run until the ankle stops hurting.

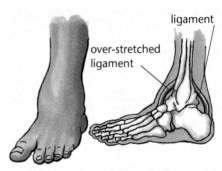

Omar's twisted ankle has started to swell up and bruise.

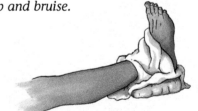

Baljeet raised Omar's leg and put a wet cold towel on it to reduce swelling.

A firm bandage supports Omar's ankle but doesn't stop blood flowing to his toes.

◼ Strains

Jenny has strained her thigh playing hockey. A <u>strain</u> is an injury to a muscle. Strains are common sports injuries caused by sudden or awkward movements (like stopping and turning). Jenny needs similar first aid to Omar.

5 Is a 'pulled muscle' a sprain or a strain?

6 Write down <u>three</u> things Jenny should do to help her strained thigh get better.

◼ Muscle teamwork

Muscles make your body move by pulling on bones that are held to other bones at joints.

You need to be able to bend and straighten your arm at your elbow. For this you have two muscles, your biceps and triceps.

Most joints are worked by pairs of muscles called **antagonistic** pairs. One muscle bends the joint, the other straightens it. This is because muscles can only make your body move when they shorten or **contract**.

The diagram shows how these muscles work.

7 What connects muscles to bones?

8 Copy and complete the sentences.

To bend your arm, your biceps _____ and your triceps _____. To straighten your arm, your _____ contracts and your _____ relaxes.

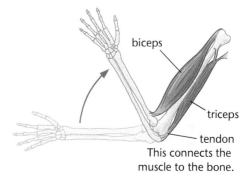

biceps
triceps
tendon
This connects the muscle to the bone.

Your biceps contracts to bend your arm. Your triceps **relaxes** *to let this happen.*

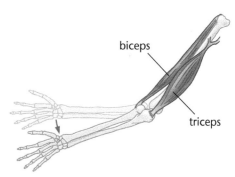

biceps
triceps

Your triceps contracts to straighten your arm. Your biceps relaxes to let this happen.

WHAT YOU NEED TO REMEMBER (Copy and complete using the **key words**)

Take care when you exercise

Your bones _____ and _____ parts of your body.

The _____ between bones let you move. Muscles cause movement when they _____. Muscles are in pairs called _____ pairs. When one muscle of a pair contracts, the other _____.

You need to be able to label a drawing of the main parts of the skeleton (page 46).

More about muscles: CORE+ C2.17

C2.9 Why you need to keep clean

The diseases you have studied on earlier pages only affect the <u>inside</u> of your body.
Viruses only live <u>inside</u> your cells.

Bacteria and fungi grow best in **warm**, **moist** places where there is plenty of **food**.
So, some grow on the <u>outside</u> as well as in the <u>inside</u> of your body.

1 Write down <u>three</u> things that bacteria and fungi need.

2 Look at the pictures.
Then copy and complete the table.

Type of microbe	Disease
viruses	
	tooth decay
fungi	

You get cold sores by <u>contact</u> with an infected person. The bacteria that cause tooth decay and the fungi that cause athlete's foot are **everywhere**.
All you can do is make it **hard** for them to grow on <u>you</u>.

3 Tony's friend has cold sores. What can Tony do so that he doesn't catch the virus from his friend?

4 Liz got athlete's foot. Her doctor told her to be more careful about drying between her toes.
Why did the doctor say that?

REMEMBER from page 21

Bacteria, viruses and some fungi are microbes.

Some microbes cause disease.

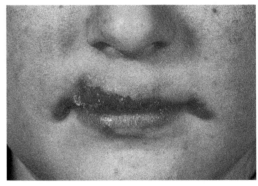

Herpes viruses cause cold sores.

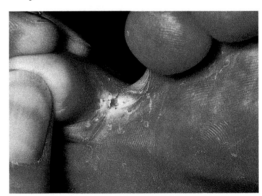

The athlete's foot fungus feeds and grows on damp skin.

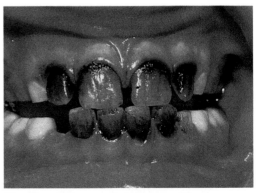

The dye shows up the plaque of large numbers of bacteria. These bacteria cause tooth decay.

Protecting your skin

Washing removes sweat, grease and some bacteria. Anti-perspirants stop you sweating. Deodorants make bacteria grow more slowly.

5 (a) Describe <u>three</u> things that you can do to make sure that you don't smell sweaty.

(b) Which <u>one</u> of these also helps to prevent spots?

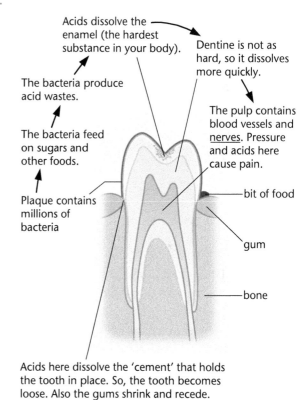

Fresh sweat does not smell. Bacteria living in it cause the smell (BO – body odour).

blocked opening of grease gland

pus in the spot contains dead bacteria and white blood cells

sweat gland

grease gland

Protecting your teeth

When you clean your teeth, you:

- brush sticky plaque off them;
- get rid of bits of food;
- rinse out dissolved food substances.

The diagram shows why you need to get rid of these things.

6 Write down <u>three</u> conditions in your mouth which are good for bacteria.

7 Copy and complete the chart.

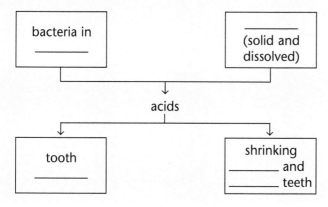

bacteria in _____

_____ (solid and dissolved)

acids

tooth _____

shrinking _____ and _____ teeth

Acids dissolve the enamel (the hardest substance in your body).

Dentine is not as hard, so it dissolves more quickly.

The bacteria produce acid wastes.

The pulp contains blood vessels and <u>nerves</u>. Pressure and acids here cause pain.

The bacteria feed on sugars and other foods.

bit of food

Plaque contains millions of bacteria

gum

bone

Acids here dissolve the 'cement' that holds the tooth in place. So, the tooth becomes loose. Also the gums shrink and recede.

WHAT YOU NEED TO REMEMBER (Copy and complete using the **key words**)

Why you need to keep clean

Viruses only live inside cells. Bacteria and fungi live in _____ , _____ places where there is a supply of _____ . You can't avoid microbes because they are _____ . But you can make it _____ for them to grow.

C2.10 Self-defence

Your body defends itself against microbes such as bacteria and viruses all the time, even in your sleep.

White blood cells destroy the microbes that cause disease. Some white blood cells **digest** the microbes. Others make **antibodies** which destroy them in other ways. Usually after a few days of being ill, the white blood cells kill enough microbes for you to start feeling better.

1 How do white blood cells 'eat' microbes?

Immunisation

Once you have had a disease, you don't normally catch it again. We say that you are <u>immune</u> to it. You can also become immune to a disease by being <u>immunised</u> against it. For example, most children in the UK are immunised against tuberculosis (TB). The diagram shows how a TB jab works.

2 (a) Why do we have jabs?

(b) How does a TB jab work?

 Find out the diseases that children in the UK are immunised against and at what ages this happens.

Antibiotics

If you don't have a TB jab and you catch TB, your body finds it difficult to kill the bacteria. Medicines called **antibiotics** can help. Antibiotics can kill **bacteria** but they can't kill viruses such as those that cause flu (influenza).

3 Why can antibiotics help to cure TB but not flu?

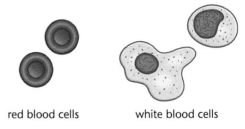
red blood cells   white blood cells

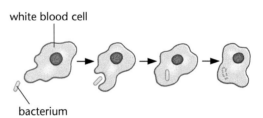
white blood cell

bacterium

A white blood cell surrounds and digests a bacterium.

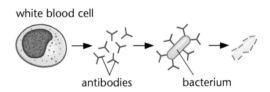
white blood cell

antibodies   bacterium

A white blood cell makes antibodies to destroy a bacterium.

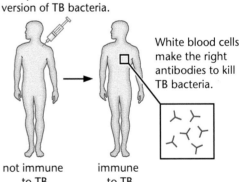
A TB jab contains a weak version of TB bacteria.

White blood cells make the right antibodies to kill TB bacteria.

not immune to TB   immune to TB

Immunisation.

WHAT YOU NEED TO REMEMBER (Copy and complete using the **key words**)

Self-defence

Some of your white blood cells make _____ to destroy microbes, others _____ microbes. Your white blood cells make new kinds of antibodies when you are infected by, or immunised against, a new disease. _____ are drugs which kill _____ in your body.

C2.11 Smoking and health

People who smoke tobacco breathe a mixture of chemicals into their **lungs**. These chemicals harm them in many different ways.

Nicotine

Nicotine causes addiction to cigarette smoking. It increases the smoker's heart rate and blood pressure which can lead to heart disease.

Cilia are tiny hairs that clean dirt and microbes from the lungs. Nicotine paralyses cilia and stops them from working. This makes smokers cough.

Coughing damages the **air sacs** in smokers' lungs so that they can't absorb oxygen so well.

Carbon monoxide

Carbon monoxide is a poison that is carried instead of oxygen in the red blood cells. Smokers carry less oxygen in their blood and this can cause damage to their heart.

Tar

Tar contains chemicals that cause cancer. 90% of deaths from lung cancer are due to smoking.

1 Why do smokers cough?

2 Which <u>two</u> chemicals in cigarette smoke cause heart disease?

3 What substance in cigarette smoke causes cancer?

4 Write down <u>two</u> reasons why smokers have less oxygen in their blood.

5 (a) Write down <u>two</u> things that can cause bronchitis.

   (b) Why are smokers more likely to get bronchitis?

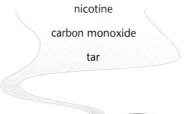

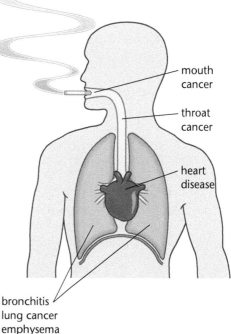

nicotine

carbon monoxide

tar

mouth cancer

throat cancer

heart disease

bronchitis
lung cancer
emphysema

DID YOU KNOW?

<u>Bronchitis</u> affects your lungs and bronchial tubes. They make too much mucus because of dirt or microbes in your lungs. Smokers are 50 times more likely to get bronchitis than non-smokers.

<u>Emphysema</u> makes you short of breath. This happens when smoke or dust damages the air sacs in your lungs.

WHAT YOU NEED TO REMEMBER (Copy and complete using the **key words**)

Smoking and health

Coughing damages the _____ _____ in your lungs. Nicotine paralyses the _____ which normally help to keep dirt and microbes out of your _____.
These things mean your lungs do not work as well if you smoke.

C2.12 Vitamin tablets

You need **vitamins** and **minerals** to stay healthy. If you eat a **balanced** diet, you get enough vitamins and minerals. Many people don't eat a healthy diet so they take vitamin tablets (but you can get too much of a good thing). You can actually **poison** yourself by taking too many.

Arctic explorers used to eat polar bear liver. Some of them died.

1 What could the explorers have died from?

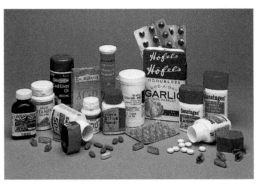

There are many different vitamin and mineral tablets.

Doctors found out that arctic explorers were poisoned by the large amount of vitamin D in the polar bear liver they had eaten.

■ Recommended daily allowance

The correct amount of a vitamin to eat in one day to be healthy is called your <u>recommended daily allowance</u> (RDA). If you decide to take vitamin tablets, watch out that they do not add up to more than the RDA for vitamin A and D.

2 (a) What is the RDA for vitamin A?

(b) What is the RDA for vitamin D?

Too much vitamin D over a period of months can damage your kidneys and blood vessels.

Too much vitamin A causes weight loss, irritability, cracked skin and weakened bones.

Ben takes a cod-liver oil capsule and a multi-vitamin tablet every day.

3 (a) What is Ben's total daily intake of vitamin A in addition to what he gets from his food?

(b) What is his total daily intake of vitamin D in addition to what he gets from his food?

(c) What advice would you give Ben?

multi-vitamin and iron tablets

In each tablet:		RDA
Vitamin A	800 µg	100%
Vitamin B₁₂	1 µg	100%
Vitamin C	60 mg	100%
Vitamin D	5 µg	100%
Vitamin E	10 mg	100%
Iron	14 mg	100%

In each capsule		RDA
Vitamin A	800 µg	100%
Vitamin D	5 µg	100%

mg (milligram) = $\frac{1}{1000}$ of a gram

µg (microgram) = $\frac{1}{1000}$ of a milligram

cod-liver oil

WHAT YOU NEED TO REMEMBER (Copy and complete using the **key words**)

Vitamin tablets

To stay healthy you need _____ and _____.
Some people who don't eat a _____ diet take vitamin tablets.
Too much vitamin A or D can _____ you.
Revise the main vitamins and minerals (pages 56–57).

C2.13 More about enzymes

Enzymes **speed up** chemical reactions but do not get used up. We say that they are **catalysts**.

Enzymes are proteins. Cells in your body make many **different** kinds of enzyme. Each enzyme speeds up a different chemical reaction in your body.

■ Enzymes do different jobs

Sometimes our bodies <u>break down</u> large molecules in stages. A different enzyme is needed for each stage.

$$\text{starch} \xrightarrow[\text{(amylase)}]{\text{enzyme 1}} \text{maltose} \xrightarrow[\text{(maltase)}]{\text{enzyme 2}} \begin{array}{c}\text{glucose}\\\text{(sugar)}\end{array}$$

1 (a) Are amylase and maltase carbohydrases, lipases or proteases?

(b) Our bodies break proteins down into chains of amino acids called peptides, then into amino acids. Draw a diagram to show this protein breakdown.

Cells also use enzymes to build up large molecules.

$$\text{amino acids} \xrightarrow{\text{enzymes}} \text{proteins}$$

■ Enzymes can work at different speeds

Certain things affect how fast an enzyme works (its **rate**). One of these is **temperature**.

2 Look at the table.

(a) What broke down the starch?

(b) What is starch broken down into?

3 What effect does increasing the temperature from 15 °C to 30 °C have on the rate at which the enzyme works?

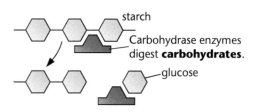

starch
Carbohydrase enzymes digest **carbohydrates**.
glucose

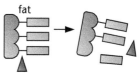

fat

Lipase enzymes digest **fats**.

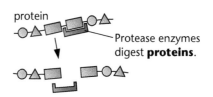

protein
Protease enzymes digest **proteins**.

Time (minutes)	0	5	10	15
Starch and water at 15 °C	✓	✓	✓	✓
Starch and amylase at 15 °C	✓	✓	✓	✗
Starch and amylase at 30 °C	✓	✗	✗	✗
Starch and boiled amylase at 30 °C	✓	✓	✓	✓

✓ = starch still in tube (so it hasn't been digested)
✗ = no starch left in tube (so it has been digested)

4 What effect does boiling have on the enzyme?

5 Why did Carla set up a tube with starch and water only?

WHAT YOU NEED TO REMEMBER (Copy and complete using the **key words**)

More about enzymes

Enzymes are _____. They _____ _____ chemical reactions.

Different enzymes speed up _____ reactions.

Carbohydrases digest _____. Proteases digest _____. Lipases digest _____.

The _____ at which an enzyme work depends on certain conditions, for example _____.

C2.14 Born athletes

Top athletes are born with an ability to take in and use oxygen at a much faster rate than most other people. We say that they <u>inherit</u> this ability.

There is a limit to how much any athlete can improve by training.

1 Write down <u>three</u> parts of her body that an athlete improves when she trains.

2 Even if they train, some athletes will never become <u>top</u> athletes. Why is this?

When cells respire, they use **oxygen** and produce carbon dioxide.

3 Copy and complete the word equation for respiration.

glucose + _____ → _____ _____ + **water** + ⭐**energy**

The sports scientist in the picture is trying to find out if the young athlete could become a top athlete. She is measuring the amount of a gas that the athlete's lungs put into the air he breathes out.

4 Write down the name of the <u>gas</u> in the air she is measuring.

5 She will know from her measurements how fast the athlete's body is taking in and using oxygen. Explain this as fully as you can.

6 How will she know whether he could become a top athlete or not?

This athlete's heart, lungs and muscles work better since she started training.

DID YOU KNOW?

The air we breathe in contains hardly any carbon dioxide.

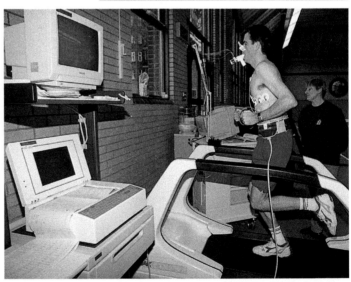

WHAT YOU NEED TO REMEMBER (Copy and complete using the **key words**)

Born athletes

The word equation for the respiration of glucose is:

_____ + _____ → carbon dioxide + _____ + _____

C2.15 How to get a good exchange rate

Substances are going in and out of your blood all the time. Some substances are exchanged between your blood and your cells. Other **exchanges** are with the environment, for example the air.

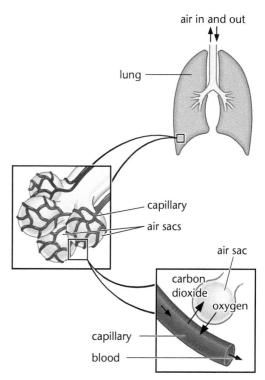

Exchanges in your lungs

Your **lungs** are organs that carry out gas exchange.

1 What gas moves from the air in your lungs into your blood?

2 What gas moves from the blood to the air in your lungs?

Your lungs are made of tiny air sacs. There are thousands of air sacs so gas exchange can occur over a large area. (The total **surface area** inside your lungs is about the size of a tennis court.) Air sacs are covered by many capillaries carrying blood to make sure that lots of oxygen goes into the blood.

3 Write down <u>two</u> reasons why your lungs are good at taking in oxygen.

Exchanges in your small intestine

Your **small intestine** is part of your digestive system. It is here that you absorb digested food into your blood. The food has to pass through the lining of your intestine. So the greater the surface area of your intestines, the more food you can absorb.

4 Why does your small intestine have villi?

5 Why do the villi have lots of capillaries inside them?

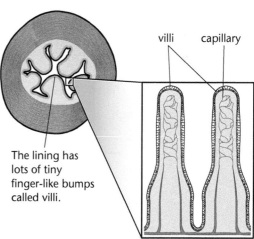

Cross-section of the small intestine.

WHAT YOU NEED TO REMEMBER (Copy and complete using the **key words**)

How to get a good exchange rate

Organs where _____ take place have a good blood supply and a large

_____ _____.

Examples are your _____ and _____ _____.

C2.16 Capillaries in action

Capillaries are very small and thin. The walls are only **one cell** thick so that substances move easily in and out.

Glucose and oxygen leave the blood from capillaries, and waste like carbon dioxide goes in. A waste product called urea is made in liver cells. So, this also goes into the blood in the liver. Each substance moves from where there is a lot of it (high concentration) to where there is only a little (low concentration).

We say that the substances **diffuse** from where there is a high concentration to where there is a low concentration.

1 What is the job of capillaries?

2 What two substances do the cells need that the capillaries carry?

3 What two waste substances do the capillaries carry away?

Oxygen and glucose don't go straight from capillaries to cells. First, they diffuse into the tissue fluid that surrounds the cells. Then they diffuse into the cells.

4 Copy and complete the sentence.

Carbon dioxide diffuses from cells into _____ _____ and then into _____.

5 Copy the table. Then complete it using these words:

low, medium, high.

	Concentration of substance	
	carbon dioxide	oxygen
in cells		
in tissue fluid		
in capillaries		

REMEMBER from page 144

Capillaries are the smallest blood vessels in your body. The blood in capillaries brings substances to cells and takes away waste.

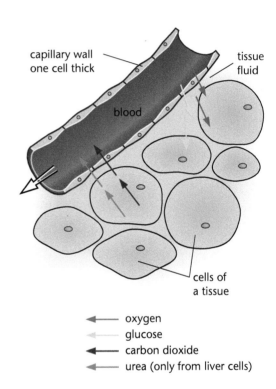

capillary wall
one cell thick

tissue fluid

blood

cells of a tissue

⟵ oxygen
⟵ glucose
⟵ carbon dioxide
⟵ urea (only from liver cells)

REMEMBER from page 108

A tissue is a group of similar cells.

WHAT YOU NEED TO REMEMBER (Copy and complete using the **key words**)

Capillaries in action

Substances pass between the blood and the tissues through capillary walls.
They _____ in and out easily because capillary walls are only _____ _____ thick.

C2.17 Different athletes for different events

Everyone looks different. This is partly due to <u>inheritance</u> and partly due to <u>environment</u>.

Inheritance

Part of how you look comes from your parents, for example, your eye colour or the shape of your nose. We say that these features are <u>inherited</u>.

1 Write down two things about how you look that you could have inherited.

Your muscles have a mixture of fast and slow twitch fibres in them. The mixture you have is inherited. Fast twitch muscles work quickly for a short time and slow twitch muscles work more slowly but can work for a lot longer.

Nathan and Yasir are in the school athletics team. Yasir runs the 100 m sprint. Nathan runs the 5000 m long distance race.

2 What sort of muscle fibres do you think Nathan has inherited most of to be good at long distance running?

3 Could Nathan ever be a good sprinter?

Environment

You can change part of how you look. For example, you can change your weight by what you eat or your hair by cutting or dyeing it.

To be a good athlete, you need to train regularly to improve your speed, strength and stamina.

4 Nathan sometimes avoids training. He says he is a born long distance runner so he doesn't need to train. Do you agree?

Example of inherited features.

Yasir

Nathan

100 m sprinter

5000 m long distance runner

daughter

mother

An example of the environmental effect. The daughter did not inherit big muscles. She got them through training.

WHAT YOU NEED TO REMEMBER

Different athletes for different events

You need to know examples of variation due to inheritance and variation due to environment.

C3.1 Daily and seasonal change

The **temperature** and the amount of **light** vary according to the time of day and the **season** of the year.

We see different animals at different times of the day.

We see different animals and plants at different times of the year (seasons).

The animals and plants on these pages were all seen in Sandra's garden. But they were not all seen at the same time.

Butterflies feed during the day.

Owls see well in dim light. They feed at night, so we say that they are <u>nocturnal</u>.

■ Animals of the night

Look at the pictures.

1 **(a)** Write down the name of <u>one</u> animal seen at night.

   (b) Describe and explain <u>one</u> way this animal is adapted for hunting in dim light.

2 What do we call animals which are active at night?

It can be hard to find food in winter.

■ Animals in winter

Food is harder to find in winter. So animals eat more than they need during the summer and store it in their bodies as fat.

3 **(a)** Copy and complete the table.

Animal	Why it needs to store food
rabbit	
hedgehog	
willow warbler	

   (b) Which of these animals won't Sandra see moving around in her garden in the winter? Give reasons for your answers.

During hibernation, hedgehogs use up the fat stored in their bodies.

Willow warblers need to store fat. This provides the energy they need to migrate to warmer countries.

Plants in winter

In winter it is cold. There can be frost and snow. The days are short and it is rarely bright or sunny. But plants with green leaves can still make some food.

Plants must be able to survive the changing seasons. We say they are **adapted** to do this.

Different plants are adapted to the changing seasons in different ways.

The picture shows Sandra's garden. Only one kind of plant in her garden can make food in winter.

4 (a) Write down the name of this plant.

(b) Explain why you chose it.

The other plants must use stored food to stay alive. They also use this food to grow new leaves in the spring.

5 Look again at the picture of Sandra's garden. Then copy and complete the table.

Plant	What it is like in winter
	bulb under the ground
	its twigs have no leaves
	only the seeds are alive
	it has green leaves

6 Copy and complete the sentence.

Most plants use _____ food to survive the _____ and to grow new _____ in the spring.

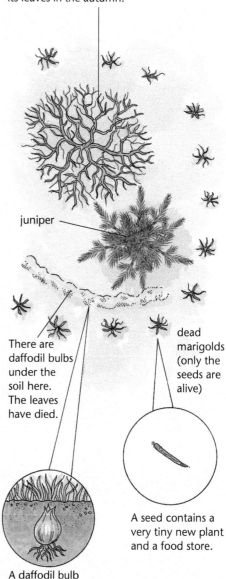

Sandra's garden – a birds-eye view.

A cherry tree is deciduous. This means that it loses its leaves in the autumn.

juniper

There are daffodil bulbs under the soil here. The leaves have died.

dead marigolds (only the seeds are alive)

A seed contains a very tiny new plant and a food store.

A daffodil bulb contains stored food.

WHAT YOU NEED TO REMEMBER (Copy and complete using the **key words**)

Daily and seasonal change

The _____ and the amount of _____ vary according to the time of day and the _____ of the year. Plants and animals are _____ to survive these changes.

More about birds and the seasons: CORE+ C3.8

Follows on from: 3.8

C3.2 Photosynthesis: a scientific detective story

All living things need **food** to grow.

Plants make their own food. Leaves take in all the things they need to make this food. The process the leaves use to make food is called **photosynthesis**.

1 Look at the diagram. Write down <u>three</u> things a plant needs for making food.

It took scientists a long time to find out all this. They found out a little bit at a time.

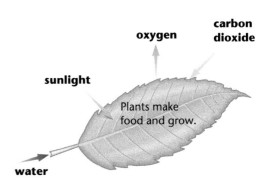

Note: Root hairs take in water. Water travels to leaves in xylem vessels.

◼ Substances which plants take in

About 350 years ago, a Dutch scientist called Van Helmont planted a young tree in a pot. For the next five years all that he put into the soil was water.

The diagrams show what happened.

2 Van Helmont thought that the tree needed only water to grow. Why did he think this?

A tree does need water to grow, but it needs other things too.

Scientists now know that a tree needs lots of another substance to grow.

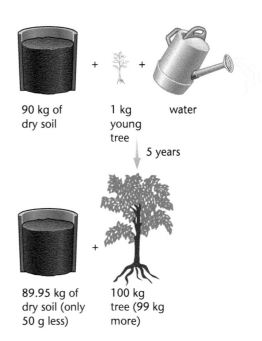

3 Look at the box on the right.

 (a) How do scientists know that trees need another substance as well as water to grow?

 (b) What is the substance called?

 (c) Where must this substance come from?

> **REMEMBER** from page 65
>
> ◼ Trees and other plants contain a lot of carbon.
>
> ◼ There is no carbon in water.
>
> ◼ Plants cannot use the carbon in soil.
>
> ◼ There is carbon in the carbon dioxide in the air.

A substance that plants give out

More than 200 years ago, a scientist called Joseph Priestley made an important discovery. The diagrams show what he found out.

4 (a) What happens to a burning candle in an enclosed space?

(b) How did Priestley 'restore' the air so the candle would burn again?

A French scientist called Lavoisier called the part of the air that lets a candle burn <u>oxygen</u>.

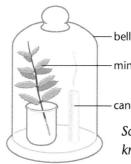

bell jar

mint plant

candle

Scientists already knew that a candle in a jar burns for a short time then goes out.

Priestley found that after a few days, the candle would burn again.

Later, other scientists realised that this only happened in sunlight.

Fitting the pieces together

Scientists are like detectives. They fit bits of evidence together to tell a story. In 1845 a man called Mayer put all the bits together and worked out how plants make food from water, carbon dioxide and light. He worked out the story of photosynthesis.

5 Copy and complete the following.

In sunlight:

■ plants put a gas called _____ into the air;

■ plants take a gas called _____ _____ out of the air.

6 Why do we call the process 'photosynthesis'?

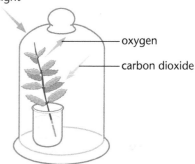

sunlight

oxygen

carbon dioxide

DID YOU KNOW?

'Photo' means 'light', and 'synthesis' means 'making'.

So 'photosynthesis' means 'making with **light**'.

WHAT YOU NEED TO REMEMBER (Copy and complete using the **key words**)

Photosynthesis: a scientific detective story

Green plants make their own _____ using the energy from _____. This process is called _____.

_____ _____

Plants make food and grow.

_____ _____

More about photosynthesis: CORE+ C3.9

C3.3 Growing tomato plants without soil

Plants have roots for two reasons:

- roots **anchor** plants in soil;

- roots take in **water** and **minerals**.

The tomato plants in the photograph are growing in water, not soil.

1 Normally, roots anchor plants in the soil. Why haven't the plants in the photograph fallen over?

This way of growing plants is called <u>hydroponics</u>.

How do plants get all the things they need?

Plants are mainly made from three chemical elements: carbon, hydrogen and oxygen. They get these elements from carbon dioxide and water.

Plants also need small amounts of other elements to grow. They get these elements from minerals in the soil.

2 Look at the diagrams, then copy and complete the table.

Element	Minerals it is present in
nitrogen	
	phosphates
potassium	
magnesium	
	sulphates

3 Where does a plant usually get minerals from?

4 Write down <u>one</u> way that you could give minerals to tomato plants grown in water rather than soil.

Plants need lots of …

nitrates   for nitrogen (N)
phosphates   for phosphorus (P)
potassium salts   for potassium (K)

Plants need some …

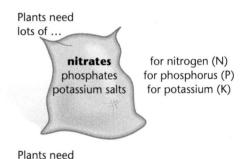

for magnesium   for sulphur
(Mg)   (S)

Some of the chemical elements that plants need.

■ What do tomato plants use minerals for?

Some parts of a plant need more of some minerals than other parts do.

5 Look at the drawing, then copy and complete the table.

Mineral	What it is important for
	growing leaves
phosphates	
potassium	
magnesium	

6 Explain, as fully as you can, why plants need chlorophyll to grow.

When a plant grows from a seed, it makes roots, stems and leaves first. Then it flowers and makes its fruit. This means that the amount of each mineral a plant needs changes as it grows.

The table on the right shows the amounts of some minerals in fertilisers specially made for young plants and for older plants.

7 (a) Write down the names of the <u>two</u> minerals which young plants need most.

(b) Explain your answer as fully as you can.

8 (a) As the plant gets older, it needs more of a particular mineral. Write down the name of this mineral.

(b) Which parts of the plant start to grow at this time?

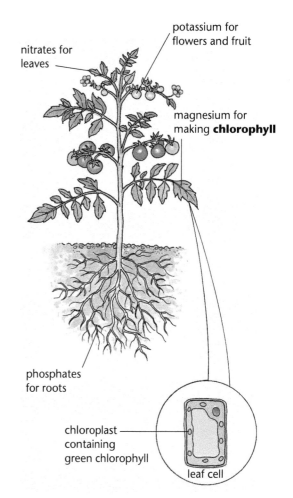

nitrates for leaves

potassium for flowers and fruit

magnesium for making **chlorophyll**

phosphates for roots

chloroplast containing green chlorophyll

leaf cell

Chlorophyll traps the light needed by a plant to make food in **photosynthesis**.

Mineral	Relative amount of minerals needed	
	by a young plant	by an older plant
nitrates	7	7
phosphates	7	7
potassium	5	7

WHAT YOU NEED TO REMEMBER (Copy and complete using the **key words**)

Growing tomato plants without soil

A plant has roots to _____ it in soil and for taking in _____ and _____.

The main minerals a plant needs are _____, phosphates and potassium.
A small amount of magnesium is important for making _____.
A plant needs chlorophyll for _____.

More about minerals needed by plants: CORE+ C3.10

Follows on from: 3.1, 3.2

C3.4 Feed the world

■ The energy chain

The picture shows what happens to the energy stored in plants when an animal eats them.

1 Copy and complete the table to show what happens to the energy stored in each 3000 kJ of grass when a bullock eats it.

Energy (kJ)	What happens to it
1000	
2000	

So only one-third of the energy in the grass is useful to the animal for its life processes.

2 Some of this useful energy is stored in new cells in the animal as it grows. Write down how much energy this is.

> **REMEMBER** from page 51
>
> Food is fuel. Fuel is used to give us **energy**. We measure energy in joules (J). 1000 joules is equal to 1 kilojoule (kJ).
>
> Food also gives us the **materials** we need for growth and repair.

1000 kJ used for life processes:
- keeping warm;
- moving about;
- growing new cells
  (100 kJ is in the materials of the new cells).

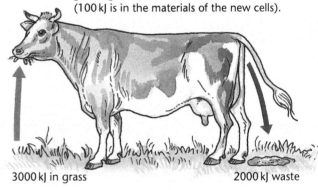

3000 kJ in grass   2000 kJ waste

3 Look at the diagram, then explain:

(a) why an animal that only eats other animals still depends on green plants for food;

(b) why all animals, including humans, depend on the Sun for food.

Green plants make or <u>produce</u> food.
So, we call them **producers**.
Animals eat or <u>consume</u> food.
So, we call them **consumers**.

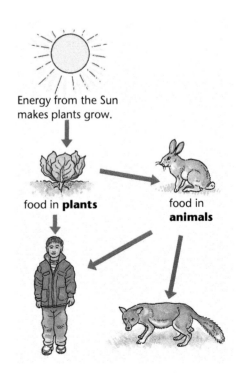

Energy from the Sun makes plants grow.

food in **plants**   food in **animals**

> Find out what herbivores, carnivores and omnivores are.
> Write down <u>two</u> examples of each.

Getting enough energy

Experts think that a person needs at least 8400 kJ of energy from food every day.

Some of this energy is for keeping **warm**. People who live in cool countries need more than 8400 kJ because they use more energy for keeping warm.

4 Why can people in hot countries survive on less food than people in cold countries?

5 Look at the map of Africa. In how many countries does the average person get less than 8400 kJ per day?

In China, most people get enough to eat. However, people are changing their eating habits. People who can afford it are eating more meat and less rice than they used to. This change in diet means that China will soon not be able to grow enough food for everyone.

6 Look at the picture. Use it to help you to explain why meat for some will mean less food for others in China.

Not all the energy stored in plants can be used. A lot of energy is wasted every time food is eaten. Undigested food and thermal energy end up in the surroundings. This is why an area of land feeds more vegetarians than meat-eaters.

It is also interesting that an amount of grain feeds more animals if the animals are kept in warm conditions. They use less energy for keeping warm and more for growing.

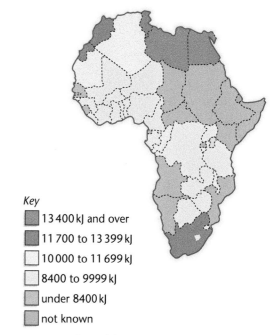

Key

■ 13 400 kJ and over
■ 11 700 to 13 399 kJ
□ 10 000 to 11 699 kJ
□ 8400 to 9999 kJ
■ under 8400 kJ
■ not known

Energy value of food eaten (per person) per day in African countries.

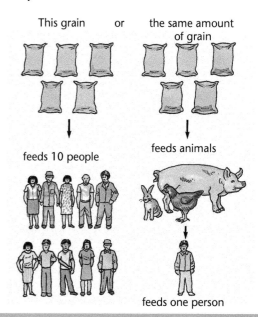

This grain or the same amount of grain

feeds 10 people   feeds animals

feeds one person

WHAT YOU NEED TO REMEMBER (Copy and complete using the **key words**)

Feed the world

Only green plants can make food. We call them _____.

We get food from _____, or from _____ which ate plants. We are _____.

Our food gives us the _____ and _____ we need to move, grow and keep _____.

More about food and energy: CORE+ C3.11

Follows on from: 5.6, 5.7, 5.9

C3.5 Food in Biosphere 2

REMEMBER from page 65

Plants need light to make food from simple substances. This process is called photosynthesis.

If people go to live on another planet, they will need to live in a space station. The station will have to provide everything they need to stay alive. The only thing that they will get from outside is energy from the Sun.

Scientists have been testing how this might work. They did this in a special building called Biosphere 2 in the Arizona desert. Four men and four women were sealed inside the building for two years.

To survive the scientists needed:

- food;
- oxygen;
- water;
- a way of getting rid of waste;
- energy for cooking etc.

1 The glass and steel building was like a greenhouse, so it let in lots of light. Explain, as fully as you can, why having a lot of light was important.

Over 4000 different plants and animals were also sealed inside. The animals and plants in each separate area of Biosphere 2 depend on their environment and on each other to survive. We say they form an <u>ecosystem</u>.

2 Look at the plan. Write a list of the ecosystems in Biosphere 2. Start your list with the rainforest.

Biosphere 2.

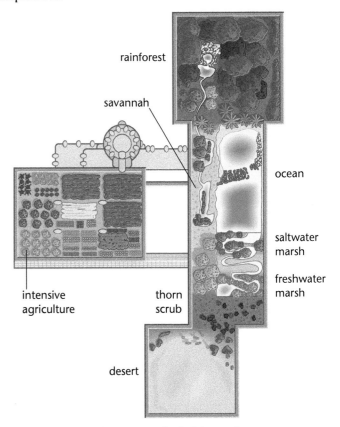

rainforest
savannah
ocean
saltwater marsh
freshwater marsh
intensive agriculture
thorn scrub
desert

Biosphere 2 is a little bigger than two football pitches.

Food chains

A food **chain** shows how the food made by **plants** passes from one living thing to another. The diagram shows a few of the food chains in Biosphere 2.

3 Name <u>two</u> producers in these food chains.

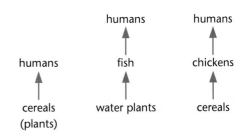

Food webs

Most plants and animals belong to more than one food chain. We can join food chains together to make a food **web**.

4 Copy any one of the food chains from the bottom of the opposite page. Then add the other chains to it to make a single diagram. You should write down the name of any plant or animal once only. Finally, write down the name of this diagram.

What happened to waste in Biosphere 2?

People and animals produce waste. In Biosphere 2, they had to do something with this waste and with the unwanted bits of plants. All these wastes contain water and minerals that plants need to grow. So these wastes were recycled.

5 Look at the diagram, then copy and complete the sentences.

Microbes break down _____ to carbon dioxide, water and minerals. Plants use waste carbon _____ and water for photosynthesis. Minerals are plant nutrients. So all the waste is used again. We say that it is recycled.

How did the humans get enough oxygen?

Green plants make oxygen at the same time as they make food.

6 Write down the name of the process in which plants make food and oxygen.

Unfortunately, the people and animals in Biosphere 2 didn't get enough oxygen or food. You can read more about this on C3.12.

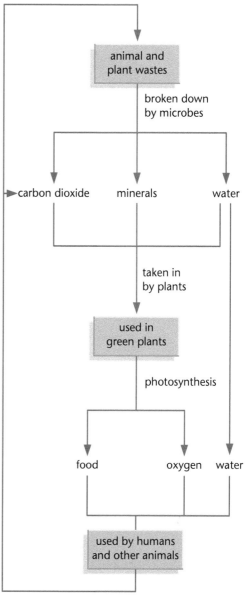

WHAT YOU NEED TO REMEMBER (Copy and complete using the **key words**)

Food in Biosphere 2

Food chains show how food made by _____ passes from one living thing to another. In a habitat, most plants and animals belong to more than one food _____, so we combine food chains to form a food _____.

More about Biosphere 2: CORE+ C3.12

Follows on from: 5.3, 5.4, 5.5

C3.6 Can great crested newts survive?

The picture shows a great crested newt. These animals are struggling to survive in Britain. To understand why, you need to know how they live.

Newts can live in water and on land. They are adapted for life on land and for life in ponds.

1 Look at the picture. Write down:

(a) <u>two</u> ways newts are adapted to life on land;

(b) <u>one</u> way newts are adapted to life in water.

■ The newt's year

Newts' bodies are at the same temperature as their surroundings.

Newts cannot keep their bodies warm enough to move about when the weather is cold. So, in winter, they find a sheltered, damp place to hibernate.

The chart shows what newts do at different times of the year.

2 During which months do newts hibernate?

3 When do they lay their eggs?

Newts' eggs have no shells. Like frogs' eggs, they hatch into tadpoles which can only live in water. Adult newts spend most of the year on land.

4 Copy and complete the following.

A newt's habitat must provide:

■ a pond for the eggs to hatch into _____ ;

■ _____ and _____ places on land so it doesn't lose too much water from its skin;

■ small _____ to eat;

■ a safe place to _____ in the winter.

REMEMBER from page 91

An animal's habitat must provide the right **conditions** for it to **survive**.

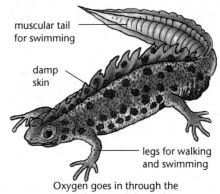

muscular tail for swimming

damp skin

legs for walking and swimming

Oxygen goes in through the newt's lungs and damp skin.

Great crested newt.

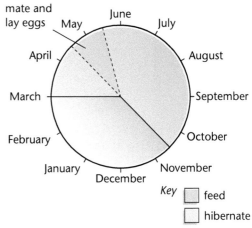

mate and lay eggs · May · June · July · August · September · October · November · December · January · February · March · April

Key: feed / hibernate

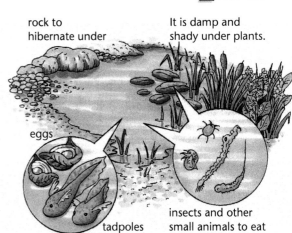

rock to hibernate under

It is damp and shady under plants.

eggs

tadpoles

insects and other small animals to eat

The first year of a newt's life

Tadpoles are adapted to get the oxygen they need from water. Adult newts are adapted to get oxygen from the air.

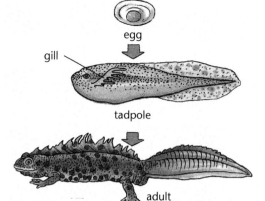

5 Copy and complete the table.

Stage of life	Takes oxygen from	Uses
tadpole	water	gills
adult		

The front legs grow first, then the back legs. The gills then disappear. The newt now breathes air through its skin and lungs.

Suitable habitats for newts

Newts need large ponds with plenty of plants around them.

Fifty years ago there were many large ponds. Most farms and villages had them.

Most of these ponds have now gone. The pictures show why.

6 Write down <u>two</u> reasons why there are now fewer ponds in the countryside than there were.

7 Adult newts can live on land. So how does having fewer ponds affect them?

Ponds are now more common in towns than in the country. Quite a lot of gardens have ponds, but they are usually too small for newts.

8 Write down <u>two</u> ways we can make new ponds suitable for newts.

*This pond has gradually filled up with mud, a **natural** change.*

*Changes caused by **humans**, for example building houses or making fields bigger, also cause ponds to disappear.*

WHAT YOU NEED TO REMEMBER (Copy and complete using the **key words**)

Can great crested newts survive?

A habitat must provide the right _____ for an animal or plant to _____.

Animals and plants are adapted to their habitats, so changes may affect them.
Some changes are _____, but _____ cause others.

More about disappearing species and survival: CORE+ C3.13 to C3.15

C3.7 The American crayfish invasion

Crayfish live in rivers. Many people like to eat them. So people started crayfish farms. They kept the crayfish in large tanks of fresh water.

Fish-farmers in Britain didn't use the native British crayfish. Instead, they brought the American crayfish over here in 1976.

1 Look at the pictures. Write down one way the American crayfish differs from the native British crayfish.

American crayfish   native British crayfish

These crayfish belong to two different species. Both live in fresh water. They can't survive in sea water.

◼ Escaping American crayfish

Many American crayfish escaped from fish-farms and got into nearby rivers. They can survive out of water and move over land. So they soon reached more rivers.

The map shows how far they spread in only four years.

2 Explain, as fully as you can, how American crayfish were able to spread so quickly.

3 (a) No American crayfish reached Ireland. Write down one possible reason for this.

   (b) Describe one way they might reach Ireland in future.

◼ How do American crayfish affect native crayfish?

American crayfish compete with each other and with the native crayfish for **food** and **space**.

4 Write down <u>one</u> way that American crayfish are better adapted to compete for these things than native crayfish.

5 (a) What do you think happens to the population of native crayfish when American crayfish reach a river?

   (b) Explain your answer.

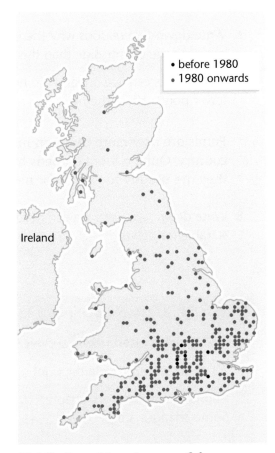

• before 1980
• 1980 onwards

Ireland

Distribution of American crayfish.

■ Why are American crayfish so successful?

American crayfish are bigger than native crayfish so they can kill and eat larger animals. They have more choice of food. If one kind of food runs out, they can eat something else.

Animals which kill and eat other animals are called **predators**. The animals they eat are their **prey**.

6 Look at the food web. Write down the names of <u>three</u> animals that American crayfish prey upon.

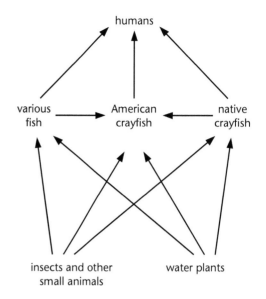

Simplified food web.

The number of each different kind of animal in a habitat is called its **population**. As the population of a predator increases, the population of its prey goes down.

American crayfish are now more common in some rivers than proper fish. This is because the American crayfish have eaten many fish and fish eggs. Only humans eat the crayfish.

As well as preying on fish and native crayfish, American crayfish carry a disease which kills native crayfish.

7 Write down <u>three</u> reasons why some scientists think that the native crayfish may die out (become extinct).

8 Explain why people interested in conservation of wildlife might agree with the message on the poster.

WHAT YOU NEED TO REMEMBER (Copy and complete using the **key words**)

The American crayfish invasion

Animals compete for _____ and _____. This affects the sizes of populations.

Predation also affects _____ size.
A big population of _____ decreases the population of _____.

More about disappearing species and survival: CORE+ C3.13 to C3.15

C3.8 Stay-at-homes and migrants

Many birds live in one place all the year round. Some grow different-coloured feathers in winter and summer. One example is the ptarmigan (say 'tarmigan'; the 'p' is silent).

1 (a) Write down <u>one</u> difference between the ptarmigan's feathers in winter and in summer.

(b) Explain <u>one</u> advantage of the change.

Robins live in Britain all year round too. They also have winter and summer feathers, but they are the same colour.

Ptarmigans need to be camouflaged against different backgrounds.

Greek robins migrate

Robins and redstarts are two different birds but Aristotle, in ancient Greece, thought that they were the same. He thought that they changed with the **seasons**. The photographs show what he observed.

2 In what <u>two</u> ways are robins and redstarts alike?

3 Why did Aristotle think robins changed?

4 Write down <u>one</u> feature which might make you think that they were different kinds or species of birds.

We know now that robins and redstarts are two different kinds of bird. Both **migrate** to find conditions which suit them.

5 Look at the map. Why do you think:

(a) robins leave Russia for the winter?

(b) redstarts leave Africa for the summer?

Aristotle was well-known for his careful observations, but even he made a mistake. This shows how important it is to observe accurately.

Robin.

Redstart.

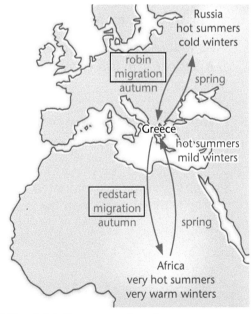

Why Aristotle was confused.

WHAT YOU NEED TO REMEMBER (Copy and complete using the **key words**)

Stay-at-homes and migrants

Some animals change with the _____.
Others _____ to places where conditions are suitable.

C3.9 More discoveries about photosynthesis

In 1880 a biologist called Engelmann wanted to find out more about photosynthesis. He knew that it happened inside some plant cells, but he wanted to know exactly where in the cell it happened.

He knew two other things:

- plants make oxygen during photosynthesis;

- bacteria always move towards oxygen.

1 Look at the diagram that shows Engelmann's results. Which part of the cell:

(a) did the bacteria move to?

(b) must be giving out oxygen?

(c) must be carrying out photosynthesis?

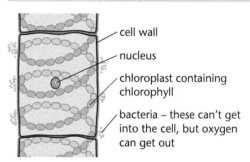

REMEMBER from page 160

The **chlorophyll** in the chloroplasts traps the light energy needed for photosynthesis.

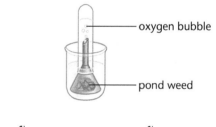

Engelmann saw that bacteria collected near the chloroplasts.

Measuring the rate of photosynthesis

A plant makes food faster at some times than others. If a plant makes food more quickly, it will also give off oxygen more quickly. So we can measure the rate of photosynthesis of pond weed by counting the bubbles of oxygen that it gives off each minute.

2 The graphs show some results. Write down what happens to the rate of photosynthesis when:

(a) the amount of light increases;

(b) the carbon dioxide concentration increases.

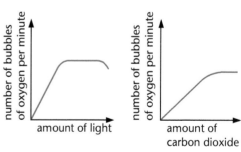

WHAT YOU NEED TO REMEMBER (Copy and complete using the **key words**)

More discoveries about photosynthesis

The word equation for photosynthesis is:

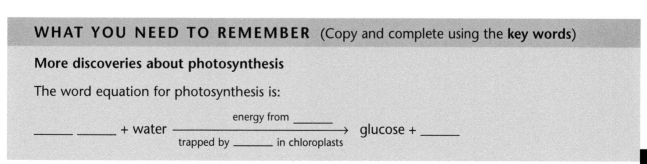

C3.10 Growing enough food

If people have no money to buy food, they only eat what they can grow. If the amount of a crop they harvest is smaller than it should be, we say that the **yield** is poor.

1 The children in the photograph don't get enough to eat. Write down at least <u>two</u> effects of too little food on these children.

Sometimes the yield of a crop is poor because the plants didn't get enough water. At other times it is poor because there weren't enough **minerals** in the soil the plants grew in.

2 What do we mean when we say the yield of a crop is poor?

3 Write down <u>two</u> things which affect the yield of a crop.

4 Look at the graph. Then describe, as fully as you can, the effect of nitrate on the yield of rice.

5 (a) What is the yield at 60 kg/ha of nitrate?

(b) A farmer decided to use no more than 60 kg/ha of fertiliser. Explain why this is a sensible decision.

Artificial **fertilisers** like ammonium nitrate are made in factories. **Natural** fertilisers come from animals or plants. Natural fertilisers also contain nitrates.

6 Why do farmers and gardeners add fertilisers to soil?

7 Write down:

(a) <u>two</u> differences between natural and artificial fertilisers;

(b) the names of <u>three</u> natural fertilisers.

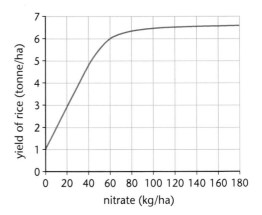

artificial fertilisers   natural fertilisers

Growmore NPK

ammonium nitrate

manure

compost   seaweed

We know exactly how much of each mineral artificial fertilisers contain.

Natural fertilisers contain variable amounts of various minerals.

WHAT YOU NEED TO REMEMBER (Copy and complete using the **key words**)

Growing enough food

The amount of water and minerals a crop receives affects its _____.

When we add fertilisers to soil, we add _____.

Some _____ are artificial, others are _____.

C3.11 Plants and animals respire

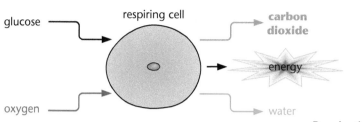

Respiration.

REMEMBER from page 63

Respiration is the breakdown of food to release energy. Most cells use **oxygen** to release energy. This is called <u>aerobic respiration</u>.

Plants use carbon dioxide and water for photosynthesis. They need energy from light to do this.

Baljit and Craig did experiments to find out if living plants and animals make carbon dioxide.

1 Baljit said that they needed to keep the plant in the dark. Explain why she was correct.

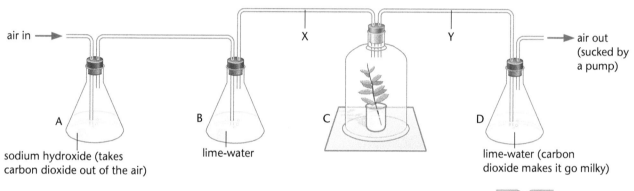

sodium hydroxide (takes carbon dioxide out of the air)

lime-water

lime-water (carbon dioxide makes it go milky)

They covered the bell jar (C) with black plastic and turned on the pump. The table shows what happened.

2 (a) How do you know that the air at X contains no carbon dioxide?

(b) How do you know that the air at Y contains carbon dioxide?

(c) Where must the carbon dioxide at Y have come from?

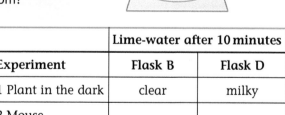

After this experiment, Craig took the plant out of bell jar C and put a mouse inside instead.

3 Copy the table of results and complete it for the mouse experiment.

	Lime-water after 10 minutes	
Experiment	Flask B	Flask D
1 Plant in the dark	clear	milky
2 Mouse		

WHAT YOU NEED TO REMEMBER (Copy and complete using the **key words**)

Plants and animals respire

The breakdown of food to release energy is called _____.
Respiration which uses _____ is called aerobic respiration.

glucose + oxygen ⟶ _____ _____ + water + energy

C3.12 Problems of Biosphere 2

Plants produce food and oxygen. Scientists thought that the plants in Biosphere 2 would produce all the food and oxygen that the animals, including the humans, needed.

The humans were at the top of all the food chains in Biosphere 2. They ate lots of different foods, but the diagram shows just one of the food chains.

As you go along this food chain, the **number** of plants or animals gets smaller at each stage. We can show this in a different diagram. It is pyramid-shaped, so we call it a **pyramid** of numbers.

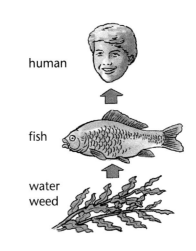

human

fish

water weed

1 Look at the food chain and pyramid of numbers that start with water weed.

In your own words describe the pyramid to compare the number of each organism in each level.

2 Draw a pyramid of numbers for the food chain:

grass → rabbits → humans

3 Look at the two pyramids which start with wheat. Which one feeds most people?

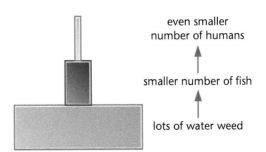

even smaller number of humans

smaller number of fish

lots of water weed

Sadly, the plants in Biosphere 2 didn't produce enough food or oxygen. The people were hungry and scientists had to pump extra oxygen in.

4 One scientist thinks that they should send only six people into Biosphere 2 next time.
Another thinks that the people in Biosphere 2 should eat more plants and less meat.
Explain why each of these ideas could work.

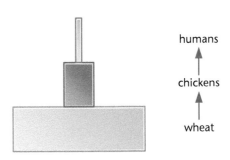

humans

chickens

wheat

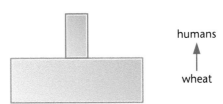

humans

wheat

WHAT YOU NEED TO REMEMBER (Copy and complete using the **key words**)

Problems of Biosphere 2

We can show the _____ of plants and animals at each level in a food chain as a _____ of numbers.

C3.13 Disappearing species

Each species of plant or animal is adapted to survive in its habitat. If we **pollute** or destroy a habitat, plants and animals can no longer live there.

Hedges provide shelter and food, so they are habitats for many plants and animals. When a farmer **destroyed** the hedges to make this big field, birds and other animals had to **move out**.

1 Write down <u>two</u> reasons why fewer birds lived in this field after the hedges were taken out.

The United Nations Environment Programme (UNEP) reports that thousands of species will die out (become extinct) in the next few years because humans have destroyed their habitats.

2 Look at the chart and table, then write down:

(a) the percentage of species of birds likely to die out in the next few years;

(b) the number of species of all kinds of animals in immediate danger of extinction;

(c) the total number of species of animals and plants which could die out soon if we don't take more care with their habitats.

	Number of species in serious danger now	Number of species likely to be in danger soon
vertebrates	602	2719
invertebrates	582	2647
plants	3632	26 106

3 Look at the photographs. Write a few sentences about what you think happened.

> **REMEMBER** from page 83
>
> Plants and animals which can breed with each other belong to the same species.

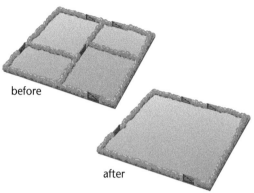

before

after

species in danger of extinction *now*

mammals

birds

fish

0 10 20 30 40 50 60 70 80 90 100 %

This is what happens when we pollute the environment with crude oil.

WHAT YOU NEED TO REMEMBER (Copy and complete using the **key words**)

Disappearing species

If a habitat is _____ or changes too much, the plants and animals _____ _____ or die.

That it why it is important to preserve habitats and not to _____ the environment.

C3.14 Survival

Only a few of the eggs in this frogspawn will survive long enough to grow into frogs. So only a few survive long enough to breed themselves.

400 eggs → 300 tadpoles → 20 young frogs → 1 or 2 adult frogs

1 **(a)** About how many eggs does a frog lay each spring?

   (b) About how many grow into adult frogs?

2 Write down <u>two</u> reasons why most tadpoles die.

Tadpoles aren't all the same. They vary in certain ways. The diagrams show some of the characteristics that can vary.

3 **(a)** Draw a tadpole. Label it with <u>three</u> characteristics which help it to survive.

   (b) Choose <u>one</u> characteristic and explain <u>two</u> ways it helps the tadpole to survive.

Some characteristics are passed on to the tadpole in the **genes** from the parent frogs. We say they are **inherited**. If this tadpole is better **suited** to its environment than other tadpoles, it is more likely to survive and **breed**. It will pass on its genes and its characteristics to its young.

4 What will happen to a tadpole's genes if it is not as well suited to its environment as other tadpoles?

 Find the connection between Gregor Mendel, Charles Darwin, Alfred Russel Wallace and the ideas on this page.

Rules for tadpole survival

(1) Make sure you get plenty of food. You will have to compete for it with other tadpoles.

   •

(2) Don't let a predator catch and eat you. You have to watch out for them and be able to hide or escape.

   •

Some tadpoles grow faster than others.

Some tadpoles have stronger tails and can swim faster.

Some tadpoles have better eyesight than others.

WHAT YOU NEED TO REMEMBER (Copy and complete using the **key words**)

Survival

Animals and plants vary. Some variation is _____.
Animals and plants which inherit characteristics most _____ to their environments are more likely than others to survive, _____ and pass on their _____.

C3.15 A problem with pesticides

Pests are unwanted animals and plants. We use pesticides to kill them.

Pesticides are poisonous. We say they are **toxic**.

Pesticides get everywhere, even to the Antarctic. Some break down quickly. Others last for many years in cells and in the environment. The ones which last longest, like DDT, are now banned in most countries.

1 Use the information on the bar chart to help you to complete the following.

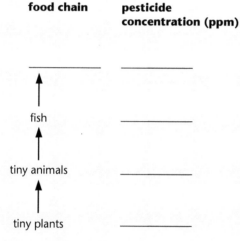

food chain	pesticide concentration (ppm)
_____	_____
↑	
fish	_____
↑	
tiny animals	_____
↑	
tiny plants	_____

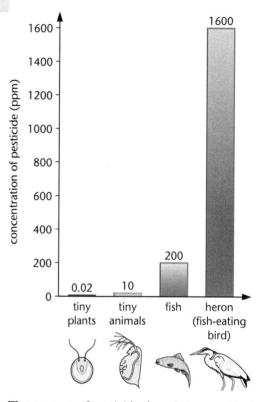

The amount of pesticide there is in a particular amount of a plant or animal is called the **concentration.** *We measure the concentration of pesticides in* parts per million *(ppm).*

2 Copy and complete the sentences.

The higher an animal is in a food _____, the _____ pesticides it contains.

The pesticide concentration is _____ times greater in the fish than in the tiny animals, and _____ times greater in the herons than the fish.

3 The drawing shows why fish can have such a high concentration of pesticides in their bodies. Draw a similar diagram to show why fish-eating birds can have even more pesticides in their bodies.

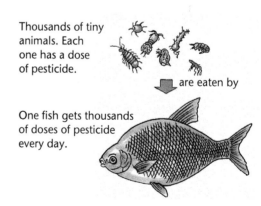

Thousands of tiny animals. Each one has a dose of pesticide.

are eaten by

One fish gets thousands of doses of pesticide every day.

WHAT YOU NEED TO REMEMBER (Copy and complete using the **key words**)

A problem with pesticides

We use pesticides to kill _____. Pesticides are poisonous or _____.

Pesticides build up in food chains. So animals which are near the top of a food chain contain a higher _____ of pesticides than those nearer the bottom of a chain.

Investigating where woodlice live and why

Science isn't just about what other people have found out. It is also about finding things out for yourself. As you read about how Hannah's science class investigates where woodlice live, you will learn about how to do science.

Hannah's class collect 50 woodlice from different parts of the school garden. They find different numbers of woodlice in different places.

1 Look at the table.
   Then copy and complete the following.

   Woodlice are mainly found _____ things such as big _____ and dead leaves.

   Their teacher asks the class to think of some possible reasons why more woodlice are found in these places. These are some of their ideas.

   Murray says 'Woodlice like damp places.'
   Hannah says 'They prefer to live in dark places. So they must move away from the light.'
   Lisa says 'Perhaps they like to stay together.'
   Philip says 'They like to be cool.'
   Cilla says 'They hide from birds that might eat them.'
   James says 'Do they find food under things?'
   Lori says 'Maybe they hide food under things.'

   These are all good ideas. Their teacher tells them that testing these ideas in natural habitats is too complicated. He asks them to choose <u>one</u> of the ideas to test in the laboratory.

   Hannah decides to put a woodlouse into an empty dish that is partly in the dark and partly in the light. She thinks the woodlouse will move into the dark.

2 What do you think will happen? Explain your answer.

   When you say what you think will happen, you are making a **prediction**.
   Scientists often make predictions. Then they test their predictions to see if they were right.

REMEMBER

The place where a plant or animal lives is called its habitat.

An animal's habitat must provide shelter and a source of food.

Where they look	Number found
on the path	0
in the grass	1
under big stones	24
under dead leaves	18
in the hedge bottom	7

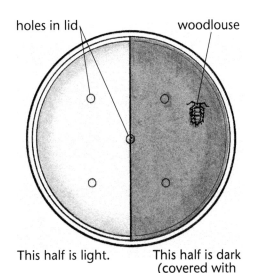

holes in lid   woodlouse

This half is light.   This half is dark (covered with black paper).

Hannah tried out her idea. The woodlouse wandered around for about 5 minutes. Then it stayed in the dark side for the rest of the lesson.

Hannah thought that her prediction was right. But her teacher said that she hadn't enough evidence to say that. She needed to do more tests.

3 Why did Hannah need to do more tests? (Look at the information box for clues.)

<table>
<tr><td>INFORMATION</td></tr>
<tr><td>There are over 40 different kinds (species) of woodlice in the British Isles. Members of the same species vary.</td></tr>
<tr><td>A few woodlice may not be normal.</td></tr>
</table>

■ Planning an experiment

Hannah finds that she has three different kinds (species) of woodlice. The woodlice vary in size.

4 Copy the table. Then complete it to show what Hannah should do.

Planning experimental procedures

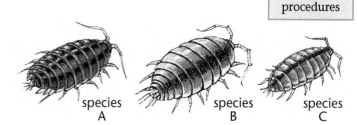

species A   species B   species C

Problem	Plan
What can Hannah do to get an accurate result for where woodlice prefer?*	
What can Hannah do to allow for the fact that woodlice vary?	
What else can Hannah do to keep the test fair?	
How should Hannah record her results?	

(*Hint: If you don't know the answers to these questions look at the table below.)

Obtaining evidence

■ Hannah's results

Hannah uses ten woodlice for her experiment. They are all the same species and size.
She puts five woodlice in each side of the dish at the start.

The table shows the results of Hannah's experiment.

Time (minutes)	Number of woodlice (species A)	
	on the light side	on the dark side
0	5	5
2	4	6
4	2	8
6	0	10
8	0	10
10	0	10

What do Hannah's results tell us?

Look carefully at Hannah's results.

Analysing evidence and drawing conclusions

5 Copy and complete the sentences by filling in the blanks and choosing the correct green words.

The woodlice moved away from the _____ side and stayed in the _____ side.
This is/is not what I predicted.

Drawing a graph

Drawing a graph is often a good way to show the results of your experiment.
You can then <u>see</u> what the results tell you.

6 Make a larger copy of the graph. One line is plotted to show you how to do it.

Plot the results for the number of woodlice on the dark side. Then draw in the graph line and label it correctly.

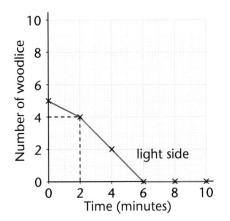

Testing another idea

Hannah wonders if all three species that she collected prefer dark conditions.

This time she lets the woodlice have 5 minutes to settle before she counts. She predicts that they should all have settled on the dark side by then.
She repeats her experiment three times, each time with a different species.

7 Why did Hannah give the woodlice time to settle?
(Look at the results of Hannah's first experiment for a clue.)

Time (minutes)	Number of woodlice (out of 10) on the light side		
	species A	species B	species C
5	2	0	2
7	0	1	2
9	1	0	0
11	0	0	0
13	0	1	1
15	0	0	0

Considering
the strength
of evidence

8 Copy and complete the table.

Species	A	B	C
Total number of woodlice seen on the light side			

9 Do you think that the results show any <u>real</u> difference between species A, B and C?

10 What can you do to be more sure that your answer to question 9 is correct?

■ Some more ideas to test

Hannah's teacher asks her to say what she has found out. He is pleased. Then he says that woodlice don't just react to light. They react to many things in their surroundings.

The teacher asks Murray to tell the class about his experiment.

11 Look at where the woodlice are in Murray's dish after 5 minutes. Write down what you think Murray says to the class.

So Hannah and Murray tested two **factors** or **variables** (darkness and dampness) that affect where woodlice live. They found out that woodlice like both dark <u>and</u> damp conditions.

12 Which variable, darkness or dampness, do you think is more important for woodlice? Give a reason for your answer.

13 You have made your prediction. If you are a good scientist, what should you do next?

Murray kept his woodlice in the light. He gave them a choice of damp and dry conditions.

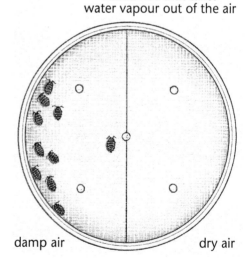

gauze for woodlice to walk on

water

substance that takes water vapour out of the air

damp air   dry air

INFORMATION

Woodlice have a hard outer skeleton which is not waterproof. So they lose water easily and can dry up.

Spiders, centipedes and other predators eat woodlice.

183

What you need to know about Key Stage 3 Science SATs

Science SATs papers look very long. Don't worry about this. Most pupils have enough time to answer all of the questions.

Easier questions are at the beginning of the paper, but you will be able to answer some, if not all, of most questions. So start with the questions and parts of questions you find easy. Then go back to the more difficult ones.

| Read each question carefully to see what you have to do. |

■ Sometimes you have to choose the right answer from those provided in the question.
Read *all* the possible answers before you choose.

This kind of question comes in several different forms.

■ 'Tick the correct box' means tick *one* box. So don't tick more than one box unless the question tells you to.

This gets 1 mark.

Which of these animals is a vertebrate?

Tick the correct box.

earthworm ☐
rabbit ☑
butterfly ☐
crab ☐

This gets 0 mark. →

Which of these animals is a vertebrate?

Tick the correct box.

earthworm ☐
rabbit ☑
butterfly ☑
crab ☐

■ Complete a sentence by choosing a word from the list.

You *must* use a word from the list.

So *gullet* is incorrect because, although it is just before the stomach, it is not in the list.

Complete the sentence by choosing a word from the list.

mouth   anus   large intestine   small intestine

Of these parts, the one food goes into before it goes to the stomach is the *mouth* .

■ From the information in the chart, choose best answer to the question.

The example opposite uses a bar chart. You have to get *both* foods right to get the mark.

Other foods such as cheese or nuts give more energy per gram, but are incorrect for this answer because they are not in the chart.

From the information in the chart, choose the **two** foods that provide the most energy.

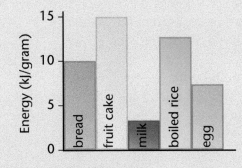

fruit cake and boiled rice

■ In some questions you will need to give short answers of one word, a few words or one sentence.

> Clues: there will only be one line for your answer.
>
> there will only be one mark for a correct answer (shown in the margin).

There's no need to write any more (e.g. *such as birds*). There's only 1 mark, so it's a waste of time.

> How does living in a burrow help an earthworm survive?
>
> *It gives protection against predators.*   1 mark

or

> How does living in a burrow help an earthworm survive?
>
> *It stops the earthworm drying up.*   1 mark

■ In other questions you will need to give longer answers.

> Clues: there will be two or more lines for your answer.
>
> there will be two or more marks for a correct answer.

These questions will often ask you to 'describe' or 'explain'. Make sure you know the difference between these two instructions.

this describes →

this explains →

> This is one food chain in a greenhouse.
>
> cucumber plant → aphids → ladybirds
>
> Describe and explain what might happen to the number of aphids if all the ladybirds died.
>
> *The number of aphids would increase.*
>
> *This is because there would be no ladybirds to*
>
> *eat them.*

■ Often in a question you will see a word or words in **bold** type. This usually emphasises what you need to give in your answer.

To give more reasons is time wasted.

> Give **one** reason for protein in our diet.
>
> *for growth*   1 mark

> The diagram shows a fish.

Your answer must be about the <u>shape</u> of the fish, so *'It is long and thin'* is also correct, but an answer *'It has fins'* is incorrect.

> How does its **shape** help it to move through the water?
>
> *It is streamlined.*

■ When asked to 'calculate' an answer, you may be told to show your working. This is important because you may gain some of the marks even if your final answer is wrong.

(a) Units may be provided.
If they are provided do *not* change them.

In a survey, 225 pupils out of 250 had been vaccinated against tuberculosis (TB).
What percentage of pupils were vaccinated against TB?
Show your working.

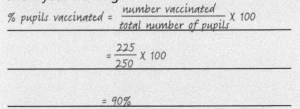

$$\% \text{ pupils vaccinated} = \frac{number\ vaccinated}{total\ number\ of\ pupils} \times 100$$

$$= \frac{225}{250} \times 100$$

$$= 90\%$$

(b) You may be asked to write in the units.

You may not get any marks without the units.

In an experiment a pupil used cubes of jelly.
Work out the volume of this cube.
Show your working. Give the units.

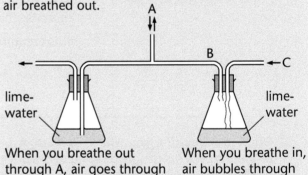

$$volume = l \times b \times h$$

$$= 2cm \times 2cm \times 2cm$$

$$= 8\ cm^3$$

2 cm
2 cm
2 cm

■ When you are asked to complete a diagram, you must do so neatly and accurately and exactly as instructed.

Use a ruler for lines that should be straight.

The diagram opposite has been completed but has several errors.
How many mistakes can you spot?

The drawing shows apparatus to compare the amounts of carbon dioxide in air breathed in and air breathed out.

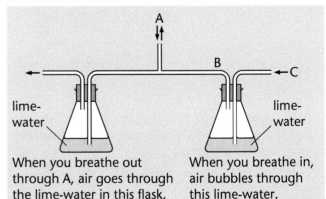

A

B
C

lime-water

lime-water

When you breathe out through A, air goes through the lime-water in this flask.

When you breathe in, air bubbles through this lime-water.

Complete the drawing to show how far tubes B and C go into the flask. Draw an arrow to show air going into tube C.

This is a correct completion.

lines drawn with a ruler

tube C goes into the lime-water

A

B
C

lime-water

lime-water

When you breathe out through A, air goes through the lime-water in this flask.

When you breathe in, air bubbles through this lime-water.

◼ In some questions you have to draw lines for labels or to join boxes.

▪ When you are asked to label a diagram, draw the guide lines accurately and precisely.

The line to the nucleus is well drawn. The line to the cell wall is *not* well drawn. It could be pointing to the cell membrane.

On the diagram of the cell draw a line from letter E to the nucleus, draw a line from letter F to the cell wall

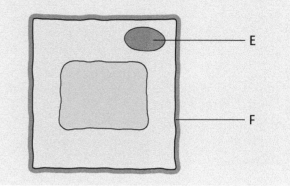

▪ Joining boxes: read *all* the statements before you begin. Link together pairs of boxes only with clear lines.

Draw **one** line from each part of the cell to its function.

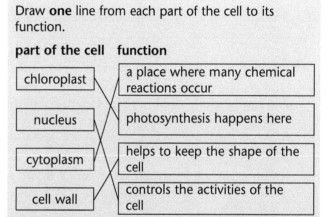

■ In all your answers, try to be as precise as possible. You won't get any marks for vague answers.

In part (a) *primary consumers* is also correct but *animals* is too vague.

Don't write down two answers when you're not sure. That way you are bound to get no marks.

So 0 mark.

Choose the answer you think is most likely to be correct.

In this food chain rabbits eat grass.

grass → rabbits → fox

(a) What do we call rabbits and other animals that eat plants?

Herbivores

(b) Explain why all living things depend on Sun for food.

Plants use sunlight when they make food in ✓

photosynthesis and they need the sun to keep warm. ✗

■ Some questions are about graphs.

Line graphs often have both axes with scales and are labelled. Look at these carefully before attempting an answer.
Accurate readings from the graph are necessary. A ruler may help.

You must also take care to be accurate if you are asked to plot points on the graph.

Be accurate! There is 0 mark for 12 or 14 minutes.

You may be asked what the shape of the graph tells you (the trend).

Cheese makers use an enzyme called rennin to clot or curdle milk. The graph shows how the clotting time varies between 10°C and 50°C.

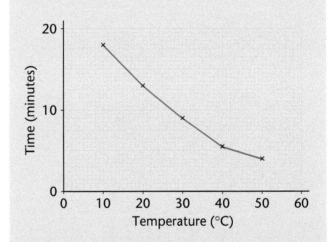

(a) What was the clotting time at 20°C?

13 minutes

(b) How does the temperature affect the clotting time?

Increasing the temperature decreases the clotting time.

■ Don't be surprised if you are asked about experiments you have not done or seen demonstrated.

Use your knowledge and understanding of scientific methods and apply these to new or unfamiliar situations.

Abid knows that an enzyme speeds up the breakdown of hydrogen peroxide. He did an experiment to see if there was a link between the concentration of the enzyme and the time it took to finish the reaction.

He measured out 5 cm³ of hydrogen peroxide into a test tube. Then he added 5 cm³ of 1% enzyme solution. He recorded the time it took for the mixture to stop fizzing.

He repeated the experiment with 2%, 3% and 4% enzyme solutions.

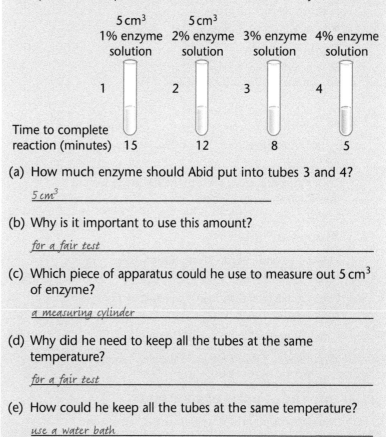

(a) How much enzyme should Abid put into tubes 3 and 4?

5 cm³

(b) Why is it important to use this amount?

for a fair test

(c) Which piece of apparatus could he use to measure out 5 cm³ of enzyme?

a measuring cylinder

(d) Why did he need to keep all the tubes at the same temperature?

for a fair test

(e) How could he keep all the tubes at the same temperature?

use a water bath

Remember that if you have some time left, go back to try any difficult parts of questions that you left and to check your answers for careless mistakes.

'What you need to remember' completed passages

LIVING THINGS

1.1 What can living things do?

All animals:

- **move**, **sense** and **grow**;
- take in **food** and **oxygen**;
- get rid of **waste**;
- and **reproduce**.

We call these things **life processes**.

1.2 Is it alive?

Some things have never been **alive**. We say they are **non-living**.

They sometimes show some of the life processes, but they don't show **all** of them.

1.3 Plants are alive

Plants, like animals, are living things. They **reproduce**, **grow**, **sense**, **move** and get rid of **waste**.

Plants make their own food using **energy** from sunlight and **nutrients** from the soil and air.

Different parts of a plant do different **jobs**.

The different parts of a plant are called **organs**.

1.4 Important parts of your body

The different parts of your body are called **organs**. These work together in groups called organ **systems**.

Some organ systems in your body

Organ system	What it does
circulatory system	carries food, oxygen and wastes around your body
nervous system	tells you what's happening around you
digestive system	breaks down food so your body can use it

You should be able to name the organs belonging to each organ system in the table.

1.5 The smallest parts of animals and plants

All plants and animals are made up of tiny bits called cells.

All cells have:

- a **nucleus** which controls what happens in a cell;
- **cytoplasm** where most chemical reactions take place;
- a **cell membrane** which controls what goes in and out of a cell.

Plant cells also have a cell **wall** and a **vacuole**.

1.6 Microbes

Microbes are everywhere. They are so **small** we need a **microscope** to see them.

Some microbes are useful. For example, they can break down **sewage**.

Other microbes are harmful. They can cause **diseases** in animals and plants.

1.7 Sorting out living things

We sort out all living things into **groups**. Plants and animals are two main groups.

Some living things, including **microbes**, do not fit into these two groups.

1.8 What is it?

We can use a key to sort living things into groups and then into **smaller groups**.

If we want to identify flowering plants, we use a **key** which is just for them.

You need to be able to use a key to identify animals and plants.

1.9 Sorting vertebrates

Type of vertebrate	What it is like	Examples
fish	has scales, breathes through gills, lays eggs	cod
amphibians	moist smooth skin, lives on land and in water, lays eggs	frog
mammals	hair covers the body, young feed on mother's milk	cat
reptiles	dry scaly skin, eggs have tough leathery shell	crocodile
birds	have wings, feathers cover the body, eggs have hard shell	seagull

1.10 Sorting animals that don't have bones

Invertebrates
arthropods
have tentacles and stinging cells: **jellyfish**
flat body: **flatworms**
round body in segments: **true worms**
some hard parts: **molluscs**

2 pairs of antennae, 5 pairs of legs: **crustaceans**
3 pairs of legs, 1 or 2 pairs of wings: **insects**
no antennae, 4 pairs of legs: **spiders**
many segments with legs on: **many legs**

KEEPING HEALTHY

2.1 Healthy eating

To stay healthy we should eat plenty of **vitamins**, **minerals** and **fibre**, but not too much **fat**, **sugar** and **salt**.

2.2 Born to exercise

Your heart **pumps** blood to your lungs and to the rest of your body. The **ventricles** do this by squeezing the blood. Your heart has **valves** to stop the blood flowing the wrong way.

You need to be able to add these labels to a drawing of the heart: right atrium, left atrium, right ventricle, left ventricle, valve.

2.3 Where does blood travel?

Blood circulates around your body, from the heart to the **arteries** to the capillaries to the **veins** and back to the heart.

Blood carries substances such as glucose and **oxygen** to all the cells of your body.

2.4 Your lungs

When you **breathe**, you take air in and out of your **lungs**.

You need to be able to add these labels to a drawing of the breathing system: lungs, trachea (windpipe), bronchus, bronchioles, diaphragm, ribs.

2.5 Breathing and asthma

In your lungs, **oxygen** passes into your blood and **carbon dioxide** passes into the air. We call this **gas exchange**.

2.6 How do we catch diseases?

Some bacteria and viruses can make you ill. Different microbes cause different diseases. For example, **bacteria** cause tuberculosis (TB) and Salmonella food poisoning. **Viruses** cause influenza and chicken pox.

2.7 Harmful chemicals

Drugs can **harm** you. They affect your mind and body. Even legal drugs like **tobacco** and **alcohol** are harmful.

2.8 Long-term effects of drugs

You can become addicted to **nicotine**, **alcohol** and other drugs.

Drugs can damage your body. For example, alcohol damages your **brain** and your **liver**.

2.9 Your skeleton

- supports your body;
- **protects** organs like your brain;

Your bones:
- give **muscles** something to pull on;
- have bone **marrow** to make new blood cells.

You need to be able to label a drawing of the main parts of your skeleton.

2.10 Joints

Bones let you move. Places where two bones meet are called **joints**.

When a muscle **contracts**, it pulls on a bone and moves it.

ENERGY FOR LIFE

3.1 Fuel and energy

We need energy for **moving**, **growing** and keeping warm. We get this energy from **food**. Food is our fuel.

3.2 Food for humans

Our food gives us the **energy** and the **materials** we need to live and to grow.
It comes from **plants** or from **animals** which ate plants.

3.3 What most of your food is made of

You need the right amount and types of food to stay **healthy**. You also need to drink **water**.

Most food is made of **carbohydrates**, **fats**, **proteins**, **fibre** and **water**.

3.4 What else must there be in your food?

To stay healthy you need to eat foods that contain **vitamins** and **minerals**.

3.5 Where does your food go?

You must be able to label a diagram of the digestive system like the one on page 59.

3.6 Digesting your food

In your digestive system, you break large food molecules down into **smaller**, soluble molecules. This is called **digestion**.

These small molecules can pass into your **blood**. This is called **absorption**.

3.7 Absorbing and using food

Your **blood** transports small molecules of food to your **cells**.

Your cells use some of these molecules, together with oxygen, to give them **energy**. We say they **respire**.

Your food also gives cells the **materials** they need to grow.

3.8 How do plants grow?

Leaves use energy from sunlight, **carbon dioxide** and **water** to make food. We call this process **photosynthesis**.

Root **hairs** take in water.

3.9 Minerals for plant growth

Plants need chemical **elements** such as nitrogen for growth.
They take them in as **minerals** such as nitrates.

3.10 How plants take in what they need

Plant leaves make **food**.

Leaves which are **thin** and **flat** are best for taking in the sunlight and carbon dioxide the plant needs.

The water and minerals a plant needs go into it through its **root hairs**.
They pass in special tubes through the root and stem to the leaves.

Roots also **anchor** plants in the soil.

DEVELOPMENT AND CHANGE

4.1 Making babies

	Male	Female
Name of sex cells	**sperm**	**ova**
Where the sex cells are made	**testes**	**ovaries**
Opening to the outside	a tube through the **penis**	**vagina**
Other organs	**penis** to put the sperm in the woman's vagina	**uterus** where the baby grows

You need to be able to label diagrams of male and female reproductive organs.

4.2 Growing and changing

4.3 Growing pains

Our bodies **change** as we grow. Sometimes it is hard to adapt to these changes.

Boys and girls start to make sex cells at the time of **puberty**. Girls start their **menstrual cycle** and they have a period (of bleeding) about once a month.

4.4 A new plant life

The life cycle of a flowering plant

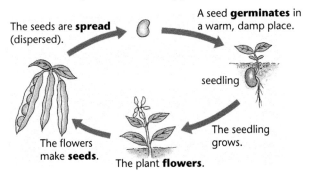

4.5 Looking at a plant's sex organs

Flower part	What it does
anther	Pollen is made here.
filament	This supports the anther.
style	This supports the stigma.
ovary	Ovules are made here.

You need to be able to label a diagram of a flower.

4.6 Making seeds

Flowering plants grow from **seeds**. Seeds are made inside the flower.

First, **pollen** is moved from an anther to a stigma. We call this **pollination**.

The male sex cell nucleus inside the pollen joins with the female sex cell nucleus inside an **ovule**. We call this **fertilisation**.

4.7 What is a species?

A species is one kind of living thing. It differs from other **species** and it cannot **interbreed** with them to produce **fertile** offspring.

4.8 We are all different

Members of a species can be different in many ways. We say they **vary** or they have different **characteristics**. But they are still members of the same species if they can **interbreed**.
All humans belong to the same **species**.

SURVIVAL

5.1 Night-time and day-time animals

Some animals are **adapted** for feeding during the day. Other animals feed at night when it is **cool** and **dark**.

5.2 How animals and plants survive the winter

The different parts of the year are called **seasons**.

In winter there is less light and it can be very **cold**.

Plants and animals are **adapted** in different ways to survive the winter.

5.3 Town and country

The place where a plant or animal lives is called its **habitat**.
A habitat must provide **shelter** and a source of **food**.

5.4 Different bodies for different habitats

Different plants and animals live in different **habitats**.

Plants and animals have **features** which suit them to the places they live.
We say that they are **adapted** to their habitats.

5.5 Surviving in a garden

Plants and animals have **features** which suit them to the places they live and for what they do. We say they are **adapted** to their habitats and their way of life.

5.6 Feeding on plants

Food chains start with **green plants**. The rest of each food chain shows what **animals** eat.

In a food chain, A → B → C means that A is **eaten** by B and B is eaten by C. We use the arrows to show the direction in which the food goes.

5.7 Growing plants for food

Animals which eat the plants we grow for food are called **pests**.
We can kill them with chemicals called **pesticides**.

We can also encourage other animals to eat them. These animals are called **predators**.

5.8 Predators, harmful and useful

Animals which kill and eat other animals are called **predators**.
The animals they eat are called their **prey**.

If the number of prey increases, the number of predators also **increases**.
As the number of predators **increases**, the number of prey **decreases**.

5.9 Garden food webs

In a habitat, plants and animals belong to more than one **food chain**. This is why a **food web** is better for showing what eats what in a particular **habitat**.

5.10 Competition

Animals **compete** with each other for **space** and **food**.

Plants compete with each other for **space**, **water**, **nutrients** and **light**.

MORE LIVING THINGS

C1.1 Cells

Living things are made up of **cells**.

Some living things have only one cell; they are **unicellular**. Living things with many cells are **multicellular**.

Both animal and plant cells have a **nucleus**, **cytoplasm** and **cell membrane**.

Only plant cells have a **cell wall** and **vacuole**, and some plant cells have **chloroplasts**.

C1.2 Working together

We call groups of similar cells a **tissue**. Different tissues are grouped together into **organs**.

Cells, tissues and organs are all suited to the **job** they do.

C1.3 Life processes

Living things can **sense**, **move**, **respire**, **grow**, **reproduce**, **excrete**, and they need **nutrition**.

Non-living things cannot **grow** or **reproduce**.

C1.4 Cycles of life

The sexual reproductive systems of plants and animals make special sex cells or **gametes**.

Gametes join together in a process we call **fertilisation**.

C1.5 The start of pregnancy

The **sperm** and ovum join in an **oviduct**. We call this **fertilisation**.

The fertilised egg divides as it travels down the oviduct to the uterus. The ball of cells sinks into the lining of the **uterus**. We call this **implantation**.

If an egg is not fertilised, the lining of the uterus breaks down and causes the bleeding called a monthly **period**.

C1.6 New plants

There are three steps to make a new plant.

1 Pollen is transferred from an **anther** of one flower to the **stigma** of another flower of the same type. We call this **pollination**.

2 A pollen **tube** grows down through the style. The male gamete uses this to reach the female gamete.

3 The two gametes join together. The female gamete and the male gamete join to make one cell. We call this **fertilisation**. Fertilised ovules develop into **seeds** inside a fruit.

C1.7 Classification

Scientists usually sort living things into five main groups or kingdoms: **plants**, **animals**, **fungi**, **monera** and **protoctists**. This is called **classification**.

It is sometimes useful to group microscopic living things as **microbes**.

There are four main groups of plants: **flowering plants**, **conifers**, **ferns** and **mosses** and **liverworts**.

C1.8 Groups of animals

You need to be able to classify animals into their main groups, just as you have done in the questions on this spread. Revise the groups of arthropods (page 29) and vertebrates (pages 26–7).

C1.9 Variation

Members of a species **vary**. Some of the differences between them are passed on from their parents. We say that these differences are **inherited**.

The **environment** also causes differences. These differences are not passed on.

A **mixture** of inheritance and environment causes other differences.

C1.10 Specialised cells   C+

You will need to be able to recognise specialised animal and plant cells like those above, and explain how each cell does its job. See also pages 68, 69, 107, 108, 109, 148.

C1.11 Organ systems   C+

Organs work together as **organ systems**. They enable life processes to take place.

See also: respiratory system (page 35), skeletal system (page 46), circulatory, nervous and digestive systems (page 16).

C1.12 Pregnancy and birth   C+

When an embryo embeds itself in the uterus lining, a special organ called the **placenta** forms. Nutrients and **oxygen** pass from the mother to the fetus. Waste from the **fetus** passes into the mother's blood.

After about 38 weeks, the uterus muscles **contract** to push the baby out. The placenta is no longer needed so it is also pushed out.

C1.13 The menstrual cycle   C+

The menstrual cycle is a way of making sure that the lining of the **uterus** is ready for the implantation of an embryo each time an **ovary** releases an ovum (egg). The menstrual cycle is controlled by **hormones** from the **ovaries** and the **pituitary** gland.

C1.14 Moving pollen and seeds   C+

Some flowers are adapted to attract **insects**. Others have flowers that let the wind reach the anthers and stigma.

Seeds are adapted to be dispersed or **spread** by animals or the **wind**.

C1.15 Changing classifications   C+

Living things have not always been **classified** in the same way.
Scientists have gathered new information using scientific instruments like the **microscope**. They have also used new ideas from the study of **evolution** and of **genes**.

C1.16 From kingdom to species   C+

We **classify** living things into groups, then each group into smaller groups. The smallest group is a **species**. We give each species a **scientific** name with two parts.

C1.17 Champion leeks   C+

We can **choose** the plants and animals which best suit our needs. We can **breed** from them so they pass on their useful characteristics. We call this **selective breeding**.

KEEPING FIT AND HEALTHY

C2.1 Illness and health

You need to look after your body.

Some **microbes**, such as viruses, fungi and bacteria, can make you ill.

Lack of just one mineral or **vitamin** in your diet can cause a disease. Too much fat, salt or **sugar** can harm you.

Some illnesses are passed on from parents to their children; we say that they are **inherited**.

C2.2 Some chemicals can damage your body

Drugs that can help your body if you use them properly are called **medicines**

Smoking, alcohol, solvents and other drugs **damage** your body.

C2.3 Healthy eating

You need to eat a variety of food to stay **healthy**. The important things in your diet are **carbohydrates, fats, proteins, fibre, vitamins, minerals** and water.

C2.4 Digesting your food

Large food molecules are broken down by **enzymes** in digestive juices. We call this **digestion**.

Digestive juices are made in your salivary **glands**, stomach lining, **pancreas** and small intestine lining.

You absorb small, **soluble** molecules of food in your small **intestine**.

C2.5 Using your food

Molecules of glucose from digested food travel in your **blood** to all the **cells** in your body. Cells break down the **glucose** to release **energy**. We say they **respire**. They need **oxygen** to do this.

Your food also supplies cells with the **materials** they need to make new cells and to repair or replace damaged ones.

Note: All living cells, including plant cells, respire.

C2.6 What happens when you exercise?

These are the things that must happen so your muscle cells can release energy when you exercise:

- You **breathe** air in and out of your lungs.
- In gas **exchange** in your lungs, oxygen goes into the blood and carbon dioxide goes out.
- Your blood **transports** glucose and oxygen to your muscle cells.
- Cells break down glucose to release energy. This is **respiration**.

All these things go on more quickly when you **exercise**.

You need to be able to label a diagram of the respiratory system (page 28).

C2.7 Keeping fit

Your **heart** pumps blood around your body.

Blood carries **oxygen** and **glucose** to cells and takes away **carbon dioxide** and other waste.

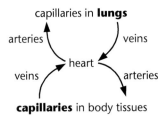

You need to be able to label a diagram of your heart and circulation and to know the features of arteries, veins and capillaries (page 34).

C2.8 Take care when you exercise

Your bones **protect** and **support** parts of your body.

The **joints** between bones let you move. Muscles cause movement when they **contract**. Muscles are in pairs called **antagonistic** pairs. When one muscle of a pair contracts, the other **relaxes**.

You need to be able to label a drawing of the main parts of the skeleton (page 46).

C2.9 Why you need to keep clean   C+

Viruses only live inside cells. Bacteria and fungi live in **warm**, **moist** places where there is a supply of **food**. You can't avoid microbes because they are **everywhere**. But you can make it **hard** for them to grow.

C2.10 Self-defence   C+

Some of your white blood cells make **antibodies** to destroy microbes, others **digest** microbes. Your white blood cells make new kinds of antibodies when you are infected by, or immunised against, a new disease. **Antibiotics** are drugs which kill **bacteria** in your body.

C2.11 Smoking and health   C+

Coughing damages the **air sacs** in your lungs. Nicotine paralyses the **cilia** which normally help to keep dirt and microbes out of your **lungs**. These things mean your lungs do not work as well if you smoke.

C2.12 Vitamin tablets   C+

To stay healthy you need **vitamins** and **minerals**. Some people who don't eat a **balanced** diet take vitamin tablets. Too much vitamin A or D can **poison** you.

Revise the main vitamins and minerals (pages 56–57).

C2.13 More about enzymes   C+

Enzymes are **catalysts**. They **speed up** chemical reactions.

Different enzymes speed up **different** reactions.

Carbohydrases digest **carbohydrates**. Proteases digest **proteins**. Lipases digest **fats**.

The **rate** at which an enzyme works depends on certain conditions, for example **temperature**.

C2.14 Born athletes   C+

The word equation for the respiration of glucose is:
glucose + **oxygen** → carbon dioxide + **water** + **energy**

C2.15 How to get a good exchange rate C+

Organs where **exchanges** take place have a good blood supply and a large **surface area**. Examples are your **lungs** and **small intestine**.

C2.16 Capillaries in action   C+

Substances pass between the blood and the tissues through capillary walls. They **diffuse** in and out easily because capillary walls are only **one cell** thick.

C2.17 Different athletes for different events C+

You need to know examples of variation due to inheritance and variation due to environment.

MORE ON SURVIVAL

C3.1 Daily and seasonal change

The **temperature** and the amount of **light** vary according to the time of day and the **season** of the year. Plants and animals are **adapted** to survive these changes.

C3.2 Photosynthesis: a scientific detective story

Green plants make their own **food** using the energy from **light**. This process is called **photosynthesis**.

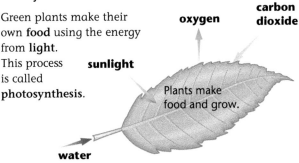

C3.3 Growing tomato plants without soil

A plant has roots to **anchor** it in soil and for taking in **water** and **minerals**.

The main minerals a plant needs are **nitrates**, phosphates and potassium. A small amount of magnesium is important for making **chlorophyll**. A plant needs chlorophyll for **photosynthesis**.

C3.4 Feed the world

Only green plants can make food. We call them **producers**.

We get our food from **plants**, or from **animals** which ate plants. We are **consumers**.

Our food gives us the **energy** and **materials** we need to move, grow and keep **warm**.

C3.5 Food in Biosphere 2

Food chains show how food made by **plants** passes from one living thing to another. In a habitat, most plants and animals belong to more than one food **chain**, so we combine food chains to form a food **web**.

C3.6 Can great crested newts survive?

A habitat must provide the right **conditions** for an animal or plant to **survive**.

Animals and plants are adapted to their habitats, so changes may affect them. Some changes are **natural**, but **humans** cause others.

C3.7 The American crayfish invasion

Animals compete for **food** and **space**. This affects the sizes of populations.

Predation also affects **population** size. A big population of **predators** decreases the population of **prey**.

C3.8 Stay-at-homes and migrants   C+

Some animals change with the **seasons**. Others **migrate** to places where conditions are suitable.

C3.9 More discoveries about photosynthesis C+

The word equation for photosynthesis is:

$$\text{carbon dioxide} + \text{water} \xrightarrow[\substack{\text{trapped by \textbf{chlorophyll}} \\ \text{in chloroplasts}}]{\text{energy from \textbf{sunlight}}} \text{glucose} + \textbf{oxygen}$$

C3.10 Growing enough food   C+

The amount of water and minerals a crop receives affects its **yield**. When we add fertilisers to soil, we add **minerals**. Some **fertilisers** are artificial, others are **natural**.

C3.11 Plants and animals respire   C+

The breakdown of food to release energy is called **respiration**. Respiration which uses **oxygen** is called aerobic respiration.

glucose + oxygen → **carbon dioxide** + water + energy

C3.12 Problems of Biosphere 2   C+

We can show the **number** of plants and animals at each level in a food chain as a **pyramid** of numbers.

C3.13 Disappearing species   C+

If a habitat is **destroyed** or changes too much, the plants and animals **move out** or die. That it why it is important to preserve habitats and not to **pollute** the environment.

C3.14 Survival   C+

Animals and plants vary. Some variation is **inherited**. Animals and plants which inherit characteristics most **suited** to their environments are more likely than others to survive, **breed** and pass on their **genes**.

C3.15 A problem with pesticides   C+

We use pesticides to kill **pests**. Pesticides are poisonous or **toxic**.

Pesticides build up in food chains. So animals which are near the top of a food chain contain a higher **concentration** of pesticides than those nearer the bottom of a chain.

Glossary/index

A few words that occur very often, such as energy, animal, plant, Sun, air, chemical and reaction are not included. Some of these words are the headings of the topics in the book. Words in italics appear elsewhere in the glossary.

A

absorb, absorption: when living *cells* or blood take in dissolved food or *oxygen* **61–63, 64, 68, 138–141, 155**

adapted, adaptation: when plants or animals have *characteristics* or *features* that make them suitable for where they live **87–88, 92, 94–95, 128, 159, 168–170, 177**

addiction: when a person can't do without a *drug* **44–45**

adolescent: a person who is no longer a child, but is not yet an adult **73**

aerobic respiration: using *oxygen* to break down food to release energy **175**

afterbirth: the *placenta* and membranes pushed out of the *uterus* after a baby is born **126**

air sacs: small sacs at the ends of the bronchioles in the *lungs* **36, 39, 151, 155**

alcohol: a chemical which can be used as a *drug* **42, 44–45, 134–135**

amino acids: carbon compounds that *proteins* are built from **60, 62, 139, 153**

amphibians: *vertebrates* with moist skins; they lay *eggs* without shells and return to water to *breed* **26–27, 121**

anaemia: disorder of the blood caused by lack of *iron* in the *diet* **133**

annelid worms: worms with soft, round, segmented bodies: also known as *true worms* **120**

anther: part of a flower that makes *pollen* **78–81, 112, 116, 128**

antibiotics: *drugs* used to kill *bacteria* in the body **135, 150**

antibodies: chemicals made by white blood cells to destroy *bacteria* and other *microbes* **150**

anus: the opening at the end of the *digestive system* **16, 59, 61, 111, 139**

arteries: blood vessels which carry blood away from the *heart* **17, 34–35, 144–145**

arthropods: *invertebrate* animals with an outer skeleton and jointed legs **29, 120**

asthma: a *disorder* of the tubes to the *lungs* that makes it difficult to *breathe* **38–39**

atria: the two upper chambers of the *heart*; one is called an <u>atrium</u> **35**

B

bacteria: *microbes* that are *cells* without a true *nucleus*; one is called a <u>bacterium</u> **20–21, 40–41, 111, 118, 132–133, 135, 173, 148–150**

biceps: the *muscle* that *contracts* to bend your arm **48, 147**

bile: a greenish-yellow *digestive juice* made in the *liver* **138**

birds: *vertebrates* with feathers; they lay *eggs* with hard shells **26–27, 121, 177, 179**

bladder: a stretchy bag which stores *urine* **113, 125**

blood: liquid for carrying materials through the body of an animal **32–36, 39, 59, 61–63, 84–85, 96, 126–127, 132, 134, 150–151, 155–156**

breathe, breathing: taking air into and out of the *lungs* **10, 36–39, 63, 142–143, 154, 169**

breed: *reproduce* or make new young plants and animals **129**

■ Acknowledgements

We are grateful to the folllowing for permission to reproduce photographs.

Action Plus Photographic p. 142 (Mike Hewitt), 145t (Richard Francis), 146l (Chris Barry), 146r (Geoff Waugh); **B & C Alexander** p. 42br, 104t; **Allsport UK Ltd** p. 54l (Chris Cole); **Animal Photography ©** **Sally Anne Thompson** pp. 82t, 82cb, 82bl, 82bc, 82br, 83tl, 83tr (R Wilbie), 83b; **Ardea** pp. 121tr (P Morris), 129c (John Clegg), 172tr (Eric Dragesco), 172cr (Jack A Bailey); **Dr Alan Beaumont** pp. 118, 121tl, 121tc, 121bl, 129tr, 158t, 172tl; **Jon Beer** p. 170; **© John Birdsall Photography** p. 47c; **The Anthony Blake Photo Library** pp. 30, 50t, 52bl, 52br, 136t; **Biofotos** (Jason Venus) pp. 103r, 104ct; **Biophoto Associates** pp.72cl, 107t, 107c, 107b; **CEPHAS/Stockfood** p. 122t; **Sylvia Cordaiy Picture Library** pp. 24tl (© Paul Kaye), 82ct (© Renee Jasper); **Trevor Clifford Photography** pp. 122b,136b, 137 lower tr, 137b, 152; **CTC Publicity (courtesy Zeneca Agrochemicals)** p. 99ct; **Lupe Cunha Photography** pp. 35, 84l, 84 2nd l; *Daily Mail* 3.1.97, p.43c (John Frost Historical Newspaper Service); **Department of Transport** p.42, the poster was produced by the Department of Transport to support its Christmas 1992 Drink Driving Campaign; **© Ecoscene** pp. 26tl (Mark Caney), 78l, 78cl (C Gryniewicz), 98t (Williams); **Environmental Picture Library** p. 177bl (Jim Hudson), 177br (Greg Glendell); **Eye Ubiquitous** p.44 (Larry Bray); **Garden Matters** pp. 64, 69l, 69r, 78cr, 78r, 93, 96b and 99t and 102 (M Colins); **GeoScience Features** pp. 18, 20b, 24tr, 27b, 89 (Dr R Booth); **Holt Studios International/Nigel Cattlin** pp. 66, 101, 120tl, 129tl, 129bl, 129br, 172cl; **Horticultural Research International** p. 162; **Image Bank** p. 145cl (Terje Rakke), 145cr (Steve Dunwell); **Andrew Lambert** p38; **Frank Lane Picture Agency** p. 88b (© David Hosking); **Microscopix Photolibrary/ Andrew Syred** p. 99cb (© 1996), 106, 107c; **P. Morris** p.120tr; **Natural History Photographic Agency** pp. 26br (Karl Switak), 27tr (Norbert Wu), 28bl (Jeff Goodman), 87c (© Stephen Dalton), 92 (© Michael Tweedie), 95c (Anthony Bannister), 98c (© G I Bernard), 99br (© Anthony Bannister), 100t (SCRI), 103l (Manfred Danegger), 104cb (Walter Murray); **Natural Science Photos** p.158c (©1997 Lior Rubin), 158b (A P Barnes); **Oxford Scientific Films** pp. 14 (Sean Morris © London Scientific Films), 24cl, cr (© Mantis Wildlife Films), 26tc (Stephen Dalton), 26c (© Michael Fogden), 26bl (© Tom Ulrich), 28t (© Peter Parks), 29 (© Rudie Kuiter), 50bl, 50bcl (© Alistair Shay), 86b (© Michael W Richards), 95t (© Philip Devries), 96c and 99bl (Philip Sharpe), 100b (Raymond Blythe), 104b (© Ben Osborne); **Phototech** p. 136c; **PowerStock Ltd** pp. 32, 108t (John Lawrence); **Premaphotos Wildlife** pp. 86c and 98b (© K G Preston-Mafham); **ProSport** 154b (Chris Wilkinson); **Redferns Music Picture Library** p.43t; **Science Photo Library** pp. 20t (Dr Linda Stannard/UCT), 28br (BSIP VEM), 33 (Martin Dohrn), 39 (Manfred Kage), 40t (Matt Meadows, Peter Arnold Inc.), 40cl (Eye of Science), 40cr (NIBSC), 40bl (Dr Dari Lounatmaa), 40br (A B Dowsett), 43b (John Ratcliffe Hospital), 47t (Department of Clinical Radiology, Salisbury District Hospital), 49 (Mike Devlin), 58tl (Mehau Kulyk), 58tr (Biophoto Associates), 58c (Department of Clinical Radiology, Salisbury District Hospital), 58b (CNRI), 60 (Biophoto Assoicates), 70t (CNRI), 70c (D Phillips), 72ct (C C Studios), 72cr (Petit Format/Nestle), 79tl (Astrid & Hans Frieder-Michler), 79tr (R B Taylor), 79b (Andrew Syred), 118bl (Dr David Patterson), 118 br (NIBSC), 132 (James Stevenson), 134t and 134c (Matt Meadows, Peter Arnold Inc.), 144 (John Watney), 148t (St Bartholomew's Hospital), 148c (Jan Shemilt), 148b, 166 (Martin Bond); **Frank Spooner Pictures** p. 174 (Alexis Duclos); **Still Pictures** p. 50c, 51, 137tl (E & D Boyard), 137 upper tr (Mark Edwards); **Stockfile** 145c and 154t (Steven Behr); **Telegraph Colour Library** p. 50bcr, 54r, 72t; **© John Walmsley Photo Library** p.84 (4 on r), 157; **The Wellcome Trust Medical Photographic Library** p. 56; **Janine Wiedel Photo Library** p. 72b; **Windrush Photos** pp. 27tl (Chris Schenk), 27tc (J Hollis), 87t (Dennis Green), 87b (Frank V Blackburn), 88c (© Richard Revels), 121br (Dennis Green).

Picture research: Maureen Cowdroy